More Praise for

DARE TO BE KIND

"Lizzie Velasquez touched me. And I'm so glad she did. (Take this in the least creepiest way possible.) Her story, her strength, and her kindness are not only inspirational to me, but to millions. And to millions more! This incredible book needs to come with every bedside table, coffee table, and school desk around."

—Liza Koshy, comedian and social media personality

"Lizzie is a true inspiration with a powerful and positive message. In a world where anyone can be bullied online, her story and insightful advice are the perfect guide to finding your own way."

—Rosanna Pansino, author of the *New York Times* bestseller *Nerdy Nummies Cookbook*

"Lizzie Velasquez is proof that the only way to make a dream happen is to believe in it. No matter what anyone says—especially the voice in your own head. She dares us to be kind to each other, love ourselves, and become the cheerleader in our own life's story."

—Lauren Zander, Co-Founder of Handel Group and author of *Maybe It's You: Cut the Crap, Face Your Fears, Love Your Life*

"I dare to be more like Lizzie! People full of love and light are the ones that are setting the bar for all of us. *Dare to Be Kind* is incredible, and I'm so excited to see what else is in store for this lovely lady! Spread love always."

—Miles McKenna, actor, comedian and LGBTQ+ activist

"Lizzie's message of spreading kindness and positivity is one that speaks to all ages. I loved *Dare to Be Kind!*"

—Amymarie Gaetner, actress, dancer, and social media personality

DARE

TO BE

KIND

How Extraordinary Compassion
Can Transform Our World

LIZZIE VELASQUEZ

with Catherine Avril Morris

hachette
BOOKS

Hachette Books
Hachette Book Group
1290 Avenue of the Americas
New York, NY 10104
hachettebookgroup.com
twitter.com/hachettebooks

First edition: June 2017

Hachette Books is a division of Hachette Book Group, Inc.
The Hachette Books name and logo are trademarks of Hachette Book
Group, Inc.

The publisher is not responsible for websites (or their content) that are not
owned by the publisher.

The Hachette Speakers Bureau provides a wide range of authors for speaking
events. To find out more, go to www.hachettespeakersbureau.com or call
(866) 376-6591.

Library of Congress Cataloging-in-Publication Data

Names: Velasquez, Lizzie, author.
Title: Dare to be kind : how extraordinary compassion can transform our
world / Lizzie Velasquez, with Catherine Avril Morris.
Description: First [edition]. | New York : Hachette Books, 2017.
Identifiers: LCCN 2017002974| ISBN 9780316272438 (hardcover) | ISBN
9781478915997 (audio download) | ISBN 9780316272452 (ebook)
Subjects: LCSH: Kindness. | Bullying.
Classification: LCC BJ1533.K5 V45 2017 | DDC 177/.7—dc23 LC record
available at https://lccn.loc.gov/2017002974

ISBNs: 978-0-316-27243-8 (hardcover); 978-0-316-27245-2 (ebook)

Printed in the United States of America

LSC-C

10 9 8 7 6 5 4 3 2 1

I want to dedicate this book to anyone who has ever felt like the sun won't shine again. I hope the words on these pages give you strength, courage, and most of all, hope. There will be a day when the dark clouds clear and the sun will be shining bright.

Contents

DARE
TO BE
KIND

INTRODUCTION

The B-Word

Bullying: It sucks.

I'm serious. That's it—that's all I really want or need to say on the subject: Bullying *sucks*!

As we address the art of kindness in this book, we must also address its counter subject: bullying. I know a thing or two about being bullied. I was bullied at school throughout my childhood, and later, I experienced unspeakable bullying online, all because I look somewhat different from your average twenty-eight-year-old. I don't want to brag, but I have pretty great hair, and I love clothes and accessories. So, stylistically, I can say I've got it going on. But physically, I'm on the smaller side... kind of on the tiny side.

If you saw me out on the street, you'd probably think that I'm a super-skinny girl. (Ugh—*skinny*. I hate that word. When I was younger, it was always used against me as an insult.) When I visited new doctors and specialists, their first concern would be trying to figure out which eating disorder I had. As

1

a teenager, strangers would see me and think I had extreme anorexia. They would ask my mom, "Why don't you feed your daughter?" Once, someone even yelled, "Eat a burger!" at me on the street.

I guess I can see why people might think that, but I am definitely not anorexic. In fact, I eat a lot throughout the day. I don't have an eating disorder. What I do have is a very rare syndrome.

But we'll get to that.

I like to think of my bullying experience in kindergarten as a big slap of reality. As a five-year-old, I had no clue how mean people could be to each other. I didn't know being mean was a *thing*! I'd grown up with my siblings, my cousins, my parents and aunts and uncles and grandparents, and everyone just treated me like Lizzie—like I was any other beloved member of the family.

That's why going to kindergarten was such a shock. That first day, it was like there was a sign on my forehead that everyone could see except me: *Don't sit by me. Don't play with me. Don't even talk to me.* No one wanted to stand next to me in line. No one asked me to play with them. No matter what I did that day, I was all by myself. The most I got from the other kids were stares.

Whatever was going on, I thought surely it would go away by recess or maybe by the time we went to lunch. I had no clue it was something that would last throughout my entire elementary school career.

And that was just day one!

It wasn't just elementary school, either. In seventh grade, I was voted princess at the Homecoming Dance. I have no idea how that happened—who nominated me, who voted for me, or how I won. What I do know is the boy who won prince did not like me. He was embarrassed by me. He didn't want to stand next to me, and when all the other couples were dancing, he refused to dance because he didn't want to dance with me. So I just sat there on the stage, in front of everyone, alone and humiliated.

The bullying continued off and on throughout middle and high school, but the worst experience of all happened when I was seventeen years old.

At that point in my life, everything was actually going pretty well. Over the years, I had made friends and built up my confidence, and it had taken me a long time to get to that point. I had a desktop computer in my room, and one afternoon I was working on my homework. I wanted to listen to some music while I worked, so I went to YouTube, which was still fairly new then. I started looking around for a song to listen to, and on the right-hand side, under "Suggested Videos," something snagged my attention.

It was a thumbnail—a little photo of a girl with black hair and glasses.

I glanced at it quickly as I was scanning the page, but something about it caught my eye. The girl in the photo looked so familiar. I looked a little closer, and that's when my nerves went on alert.

Was that *me*?

At first I thought, *No, that's not me. That* couldn't *be me.* But when I clicked on it, of course, I found that it was.

All the air in my entire body suddenly vanished—it just whooshed out of me, and I was left sitting there, speechless and trying to breathe. I had one hand over my mouth and the other over my heart, which was beating incredibly fast.

I scrolled down the page and read the title of the video— "World's Ugliest Woman"—and then noticed the view count. Over 4 million viewers had already watched this video of me, because they all wanted to see the ugliest girl in the world. It was like the entire Internet was the circus, and I was the world's most popular sideshow attraction.

I watched the video. There was no sound to it, and it was only eight seconds long. All I felt, all I could feel, was shock.

When I scrolled down to the comments below and read the first two, I saw that they were awful.

Why didn't her parents abort her?

Kill it with fire!!!

My astonishment only increased. Why had 4 million people watched such a video? And why had so many gone out of their way to post such hateful, negative comments?

Then something happened: It was like the floodgates opened, and I just couldn't stop reading those comments, every horrible one.

If people see her face in public, they will go blind.

WHAT A MONSTER!

She should just put a gun to her head and kill herself!

Kill yourself.

Do everyone a favor and just kill yourself.

I ended up reading a good two thousand or so comments, one after another, while sitting there at my desk. I was desperately searching for just one person who might have stood up for me.

No one had. Not one comment was kind. Every single one was mean and nasty.

The door to my room was open. When I looked out into the hall, I could see into the living room, where my mom was sitting. I remember looking at her and then just starting to bawl. Instantly, I wanted to hide this awful discovery from my parents, because I knew they would feel so powerless and upset. They would feel the way I felt, but times a million.

So I just sat there and cried silently. You know when you cry really hard, and you want to make those awful ugly-cry sounds, but instead you hold it in? That's what I was doing. There was a towel on my bed, and I grabbed it and held it over my mouth to muffle the sounds. I was just praying my mother wouldn't look into my room and see me falling apart.

Then, of course, she did get up and came toward the hallway. I didn't see her. I was crying too hard. But she saw me, and she came into my room and asked me what was going on.

When I told her, she cried, too—but not in front of me. In front of me, she held it in. Still, I know my mom very well, so I knew exactly how upset she was. She had no idea what to do. She immediately told me to stop looking at the comments on the video. "Close it," she said, meaning I should close the Web browser window immediately. But I couldn't do it. I couldn't make myself close the window. I just sat on my bed and kept crying.

A while later, my dad came home, and we told him about the video. Being my dad, he tried to make light of it—but for just about the first time ever, making light of the situation wasn't easy. There was nothing he could say that could make things better.

That's not normal. My dad had always been able to make things better with a joke, a smile, and a hug. Not this time, though. None of us knew what to say. We were all completely shocked. I had been bullied before, of course, and my parents had always taught me to laugh it off, stay confident, and keep my sense of humor about me. But none of us had known anything like this could happen, so we had no preparation for it when it did.

Finding that video was by far the worst, most devastating and unexpected shock of my life. As soon as I laid eyes on it and all those awful comments people had posted, it was as if all the hard work I'd done over the years building up my confidence went right down the drain. In an instant, it was gone. It was the first time I had ever felt completely defeated.

Fast-forward a decade. At twenty-eight years old, I am a motivational speaker and an antibullying activist. I absolutely love my work. I feel that it's what I am meant to do, what I'm here on this earth to accomplish. But what's most meaningful and important to me is being able to support people and their families who have experienced what my parents and I did. My viewers on YouTube who post comments on my videos, sharing their own stories about being bullied or feeling alone and unwanted, are the people I am motivated by every day.

If you look at their comments, you might get the sense that bullying is a rampant problem—and it is. So many of us have our own stories of intimidation, victimization, and pain. Bullying comes in lots of different forms. But shaking our heads in sorrow or even reaching out in commiseration isn't enough. The problem of bullying has a solution, and it's a very simple one: kindness.

Kindness toward ourselves and kindness toward the bully.

That might seem ridiculous. Kindness probably seems like the last thing a bully deserves, and treating bullies with kindness is definitely difficult to do. Believe me, I know from personal experience, since that's my approach every time I encounter a bully.

It's been a long process, but I have come to see that a culture of kindness is what we desperately need. It is the best solution to the problem of bullying, in all instances and at all levels, from schoolyard taunting to the systemic marginalization of minority groups, and even to our country's problem of violence that has gotten so out of control.

Kindness is what I have found to be the best answer to all of these issues.

CHAPTER 1

Kindness Begins at Home

The first step in creating a culture of kindness begins at home. More times than I can count, parents have asked me, "My child is being bullied—how can I help her through it?"

I can never give them an answer, at least not in a quick sentence or two, that will solve their problem. It's a tough and complicated issue, and besides, I'm not a parent. All I have to offer is what I've learned from my own parents and what they did to help me.

The way parents treat each other and their children creates their "family culture," and that culture sets the tone for the rest of a person's life. I am so grateful to my family for being the kind, loving, and supportive people they are. I am well aware that not everyone is as blessed to have had such a close and caring upbringing.

My parents have always done a really good job of keeping the lines of communication open between us. When I was growing up, they helped me feel safe enough to talk to them

about whatever I was going through, even when it was something terrible. This is essential for parents to do if they want
to help their children navigate tough social situations, both
online and in school. It's important for kids to be able to talk
openly and honestly with their parents about their lives, and
not just when things are going well. When things are going
badly is when it's most important to keep those lines of communication open and strong.

Parents define "safety" for their child in every aspect of
life—no matter what age the child is. No matter how old we
are, we need that safety net, and providing it is a big part of a
parent's job.

Regardless of the particular structure of a family, from the
first day of every child's life, their family's values and beliefs
are setting their foundation. Let's be clear: There are many
types of families, whether it's grandparents or other extended
family members serving as a child's guardians, or a single parent taking care of a child on their own. Children learn how
and whom to love—whether that's family members, friends,
or community members—at home.

I like to think of those values as flowers that need regular sun and water. No matter how old a child gets, it is the
parents' responsibility to keep watering those flowers. At
times parents will have to use different lessons and methods to instill certain principles and beliefs: Sometimes it will
be through love, and other times it will be through overcoming trials and obstacles as a family, with kindness and
compassion.

That's how it starts at home: not just with a conversation

here and there about bullying, but with a foundation that encompasses so many other things. Bullying is just one small part of the great, big whole.

At the same time, I understand how tough it can be for kids to talk to their parents about their problems and insecurities. Sometimes, kids are afraid to admit they're having problems because they're scared of getting in trouble, especially if they've made a bad decision that brought the problems onto themselves. Many times, they don't want to admit the awful things that are happening to them at the hands of their peers, because they're just too embarrassed by how they're being treated. Often, kids want to protect their parents from the pain they think their parents may experience when they learn how hurt and sad their child is feeling.

That's definitely how I felt growing up. I wanted to protect my parents from knowing all the awful, hurtful things that other kids were saying to me on a daily basis and, later, the hateful things people said to me and about me online.

My generation was really the first whose parents had to deal with their kids' activity on social media and figure out how to parent within that venue. Children are now living out their lives online from an incredibly early age, and we're only just beginning to see the consequences, which include cyberbullying, dangerous breaches of privacy, and so much more. That's why kindness and compassion are more important than ever.

The truth is, parents and guardians cannot ban their kids from being on social media, nor should they have to. Such strict limits just aren't realistic in the world we live in today. Social media is everywhere. It's a fact of life, part of the way childhood is in today's day and age. There are other ways to handle the many potential pitfalls of young people venturing online.

Lots of young kids don't realize what the Internet is really all about; they don't realize it's not just a happy place that's full of nice people! Sure, those things are part of it, but there is so much more to it, and so much potential for danger.

Aside from the various safeguards that can be put in place on the Internet or on social media platforms, parents should focus on compromise and limitations when talking with young people about starting social media accounts. For example, parents' insistence on having their tweens' or teens' passwords just makes the child feel as if they don't have any privacy. But maybe if a parent and child can agree to be connected as friends on social media, then the whole family can stay aware of what's going on in the child's life.

Of course, some children may rebel against those kinds of limits and expectations, which can also be a scary prospect for many parents. They might fear such limits will push their child away: *What if my child just completely defies me?* That can certainly happen, but that level of rebellion doesn't come out of nowhere. Maybe kids who act out toward their parents with hostility have been treated that way themselves, or maybe they've watched their parents treat each other that way.

Our entitlement culture has established that no one— children or adults—wants to be told no anymore.

Kids definitely don't want to be told no, whether it's "No, you can't have that cookie," "No, you weren't the best player on the team," or "No, you can't have a smartphone at age seven." Parents don't want to have to say no to their children. No one wants to be the bad guy.

But as kids get older, compromising with their parents on how they will approach their online life relies on their willingness to accept limits. Parents also have to remember that it's perfectly normal for children and teenagers to push those limits. That's a normal, albeit scary, part of growing up! For preteens and teenagers, pressures of all kinds—social, academic, hormonal, familial—are mounting all around them, all the time. Kids act out at those ages, and that is developmentally appropriate.

That's why it's so important for parents to stay tuned in, and not necessarily in an authoritarian way, either. Parenting a teenager isn't just about clamping down the controls.

In my opinion, the only thing that works is keeping the lines of communication as open and judgment-free as possible and equipping children to be smart enough to make their own good choices.

———

I recently met a woman named Cindy and her daughter, Alanna, who struggled with depression and was bullied at school. Alanna and her mom wore matching bracelets that were printed with a saying they loved: *You Are Awesome!* It was a simple, yet powerful daily connection that they shared. Every time Alanna looked at her bracelet, she could feel that little surge of confidence and love, knowing her mom had her back. Many teenage girls love jewelry and cute accessories, and Cindy made the effort to connect with her daughter on that teenage level, in a wonderfully positive way that would help Alanna any time she needed a boost.

Every single day, I wear a necklace stamped with the word *BRAVE*. I got the necklace from a company called All the Wire after the release of the documentary about my life, *A Brave Heart: The Lizzie Velasquez Story*. Because of the film and because of what I've been through, the meaning behind that single word, *brave*, is enormous to me. Wearing the necklace reminds me to be brave, no matter what I'm walking into. I love wearing reminders of what's most important to me. I also wear a ring with a dangling cross charm that reminds me to walk in my faith—to live according to my spiritual beliefs and remember God is always with me. My BRAVE necklace and cross ring are two of my favorite pieces of jewelry, and I rarely take them off.

In regard to Cindy and Alanna's bracelets, a person's alliance with their family can also serve as a positive reinforcement of who they are.

———

To create more kindness in our homes, it's incredibly important for parents to treat their children as they want their children to treat others. It's like the Golden Rule—*Do unto others as you would have them do unto you*—but my version of the Golden Rule isn't just about treating people the way you want to be treated. It's also about modeling kind, respectful treatment of others to show people how they can and should treat everyone around them.

As I've said, this starts at home. Parents must treat their

children the way they want their children to treat other people out in the world. Parents, after all, are the first and best models for their children in how to be a good person. That's why this is such an important factor for parents to understand—and not just for parents who want to help their kids who are being bullied. It's also hugely important for parents who don't want their children to *become* bullies.

Some parents view bullying as a way to make their kids stronger, and they don't see all the possible, terrible consequences it can have. They just see it as, "Toughen up, kid." Some people believe bullying is a normal part of childhood—so normal, in fact, that they might not even consider certain behaviors to be bullying at all.

Even I have a hard time defining what bullying is. What do you think of when you think of bullying? Chances are, you picture a group of kids taunting or making fun of a smaller, weaker kid, or shoving them, or laughing at them. That's a very traditional image of bullying, and it's certainly one version of it.

So what is bullying? A simple definition of a bully is someone who uses their strength, whether physical, verbal, or emotional, to hurt or intimidate someone else they perceive as being weaker than themselves.

Just think about that definition for a second. Think about how general and wide-reaching it is. Then think about all the little things, all the small events that happen every day that could fit that definition—events that most people would think of as perfectly normal and acceptable, not bullying at all.

When children in the same family argue and fight, people call it sibling rivalry. Maybe siblings make fun of each other, say hurtful things about each other, and even get into physical fights in order to feel more powerful. Maybe they harbor competitive or jealous feelings. Whatever the reasons behind sibling rivalry, this phenomenon may not be seen as a good thing, but it's still viewed as common and normal.

The same is true of hazing rituals. Despite the fact that many colleges and universities across the country have cracked down on it in recent years, hazing is still all too common among kids entering high school or college or joining a fraternity or sorority. This is certainly true in my home state of Texas, where many students continue to view hazing as a necessary ritual to prove they're "macho" or worthy enough to enter Greek life on campus. Even parents seem to consider it a point of pride, after having gone through hazing rituals themselves; their children grow up and carry on the tradition.

Public humiliation is also one of many tactics used by bullies. In my mind, it's no different when a well-meaning parent uses that tactic to discipline their children. As soon as a parent shames their child in public, they have become a bully.

Thank goodness people are speaking out about this phenomenon. One of my favorite videos that I've seen on the subject was made by Wayman Gresham, a Florida father who posted his own public humiliation discipline video—with a twist. Instead of cutting his son's hair in the video, he said to the camera, "Good parenting starts before he even gets to the point of being out of control. Good parenting is letting your child know that you love them, regardless of what they are and who they are, and showing them the way by example."

I loved that message so much. Mr. Gresham is exactly right: Modeling kindness, setting that good example, is the best way to teach and inspire a child to be kind themselves.

As an anti-bullying activist, I am calling for a sea change— a cultural shift. Because enough is enough. There have been too many young children who have committed suicide after being bullied. There have been too many college kids who died after a "harmless" hazing ritual in their new fraternity. There have been too many people irrevocably harmed by someone else's thoughtless cruelty.

And this sea change, this cultural shift, has to begin at home. Mahatma Gandhi is known for the saying, *Be the change that you wish to see in the world.* When I was growing up, my parents really modeled this for me, and I followed their example when I found the strength to rise above all the hateful negativity that people threw my way. That's why I believe so deeply that change starts at home.

The love that family members share is essential, and it's so important to highlight it no matter what else might be happening. This is especially true when there is something causing true, deep discord among family members—something fundamental that could cause a real rift.

It's like what Wayman Gresham said in his viral video: Parents must love and accept their children for who they are. Learn who they are, and try to understand them. Open your eyes and ears and heart; look at your child, listen to them, and love them fiercely as you try to learn everything you can about them. If you do that, you can support them in becoming fully themselves, the person they were meant to be.

In so doing, you will raise a human being who takes that open-minded, tolerant perspective out into the world. They will be able to love and accept other people, because you loved and accepted them first.

Parents who treat their children with kindness and acceptance are giving a true gift to the world.

CHAPTER 2

Hurt People Hurt People

Hurt people hurt people.

It's an age-old saying, and it's as simple and true as it ever was: People speak hatefully due to their own pain.

My dad, Lupe, taught me that from a very early age. He is really rooted in that belief. My whole family is, actually. When someone is being mean, they'll get mad or upset, like anyone else, but at the same time, they understand the other person isn't just doing it to be hurtful. It's not as simple as that: The deeper truth is that someone is only hurtful to others because they are hurting themselves.

This concept has always been in my mind, but now it's one that I'm able to put out into the world. Rather than just meditating on it privately, I now get to live it out in my work, using it as I strive to evolve our cultural dialogue.

The first time I crossed paths with Sara Hirsh Bordo, the director and producer of *A Brave Heart*, was in 2013 when I gave a TEDx AustinWomen talk titled "How Do You Define

Yourself?" Sara executive-produced the event, which ended up going viral. To date, it has been viewed well over 12 million times, making it one of the most-watched TEDx talks of all time. Shortly after that, Sara and I began working together on the documentary about my life and work as a motivational speaker and antibullying activist.

One of the people featured in the documentary is Tina Meier, whose daughter Megan was bullied on Myspace. Megan committed suicide in 2006, just shy of her fourteenth birthday. Despite her unimaginable grief and pain, Tina has turned her family's terrible tragedy into a force for good, working tirelessly as an antibullying activist.

In 2007, Tina founded the Megan Meier Foundation, dedicated to promoting awareness, education, and positive change in response to the issues surrounding bullying, cyberbullying, and suicide. The Foundation is also dedicated to celebrating individuality and acceptance of others as an important part of creating a kinder and safer world for everyone.

I can't think of better goals. And these are goals that most definitely align with my own.

During the filming of our documentary, I was fortunate enough to see Tina Meier's entire interview, which was almost two hours long. Later, the filmmakers cut it down to a short, brilliant piece, but I'm grateful that I got to hear so much of Tina's story. When I watch the film, the only part that ever makes me cry is those few minutes of her interview. I can't imagine the heartbreak or the overwhelming hopelessness Tina must have felt when she faced her beloved daughter's suicide.

I carry Megan with me every day. Since I never met her, I've only gotten to know her through Tina, but she is a part of me now and a part of my heart. She is an important piece of this whole puzzle of bullies and bullying. She is an important part of reaching a point where no one believes the world would be better off without them in it.

It's difficult to know the right way to deal with bullies— the best way to respond to them, especially when they do something excessively cruel, something with devastating consequences, like what was done to Megan Meier. The problem is that fighting anger with anger does nothing but make the problem bigger. Whatever it is within a bully that is already so hurt, so fearful and damaged, that they would torment someone so ruthlessly—striking back at them with anger only makes it worse. People who are that fearful and wounded need compassion, not aggression. But how do you offer compassion to someone who has done something unforgivably vicious?

I wish everyone, especially people who are being bullied, could understand that bullies are coming from a place of hurt—that there is something wrong not with the individuals who are being bullied but with the bullies themselves. I wish everyone could recognize, instantly and deeply, that no matter what awful things are said or done to them, they should not take it personally, because it has nothing to do with them.

If they could understand this, then they would be able to say to the bully, "I am so sorry you're in pain. What is going on in your life that you would unleash this kind of ugliness on me?"

It took me a very long time to get to the point where I could do and understand all of that. I was so nervous to reach out and talk to the people who were bullying me and try to find out what was wrong with them. But over time, I just kept thinking about that concept. Like so many others who have been bullied in childhood or adulthood, I turned it over and over in my mind. I would brainstorm all these ideas about why someone would do this to me—why they would want to hurt me. Was it me? Was it something I did that brought it on? Did I somehow deserve it?

Then my dad brought it to my attention that the person who was going out of their way to hurt me might be going through something even worse in their own life. Maybe, he suggested, they just didn't know how to channel their feelings. Maybe all they knew was hurting other people; maybe meanness and anger were all they got to see or experience at home. Like so many others, I just happened to be the unlucky one on the receiving end of their damage.

Over time, I kept realizing the truth of that again and again. My realization and acceptance of this concept came in waves, and each time, it made more and more sense...until finally, it became my automatic mind-set.

———

Dr. Bob Faris, the sociologist featured in *A Brave Heart*, was right when he said we are living in a culture of meanness. In America, it seems to be at least partly related to capitalism. Money can seem like the most important thing, the thing that trumps everything. People are encouraged every day, on billboards and TV, in movies and magazines, to spend more and more money on clothes and products and treatments to make them more beautiful and desirable, more acceptable and enviable.

Marketing firms have definitely figured out how to worm their way into our minds and prey on our deepest insecurities! It's all too easy to get caught up in that kind of thinking. The problem is that it perpetuates this false idea that people are different from each other. That some people are better, or more deserving, than others. But that just isn't true. We are all the same, and we all deserve happiness and love.

With the help of Congresswoman Linda Sanchez, Tina Meier organized a march on Capitol Hill and tried to get a cyberbullying act passed. Unfortunately, nothing came of their efforts at that time, but much later, after a screening of my documentary at the Paramount Theatre in Los Angeles, a young woman from the audience came up to me. "I was just bawling," she told me, "because I took part in Tina Meier's march on Capitol Hill. I had no idea she was going to be in this movie." She was so happy she'd been a part of that march and that moment.

She told me she was a fashion blogger. She said, "We're the worst people!" I was so surprised—she was owning it. She said that seeing the documentary made her feel that her purpose was to help make a difference in that world. Her realization made me feel *really* good.

When I think about what happened to the Meier family, I get the chills.

In the documentary, Tina talks about finding Megan hanging in her room, and she says something about thinking, in that moment, "That's it—it's over, there are no more chances to make this better." I can't even imagine. That has to be the worst feeling in the world.

As long as you're alive on this earth, however, there are still plenty of chances to make things better—for yourself and for everyone else. This can be an evolving process over time. I still deal with bullying every single day, but my approach to people's hateful comments on YouTube and Twitter has definitely evolved. Instead of responding directly to a nasty comment, I'll post a blog or a video about something positive.

In essence, that's my philosophy: I want to counter people's negativity and hate by spreading love and positivity. Everything is a choice, and once you make your choice, it's really very simple. Many people don't realize how much they can do, as far as making bad choices or good ones. Even if you decide just to make the smallest good choice, it's eventually going to lead to something great that is much bigger than yourself.

––––––––––

But not everyone gets the modeling at home that they need to learn to treat others with kindness and respect. Megan Meier was bullied by a girl who lived down the street—a "frenemy" whom Megan believed to be a good friend, although sometimes they would fight. But the girl didn't act alone. It turned out the girl's mother may have been aware of the cyberbullying of Megan Meier.

Whatever the circumstances might have been, I can't imagine why parents would involve themselves in something so cruel. All I know is that, unfortunately, this kind of thing happens. Parents are supposed to be kind and mature, yet some simply aren't. Some children learn cruelty at home and then turn that cruelty both inward, toward themselves, and outward, toward others.

Since children come from all kinds of backgrounds, experiences, and family cultures, it is especially important for schools to tackle bullying head-on. Many young people aren't getting the right treatment, modeling, or message at home, and the media isn't helping much, either. It's up to schools to be at the forefront of tackling this problem. Of course, bullying has been a hot topic in schools for a long time now, as well as in the media and elsewhere. It's something everyone is talking about, but to me, "bullying" has become almost too much of a buzzword to allow the real, deep, raw, and honest conversation that must happen about this all-too-common phenomenon.

Congresswoman Sanchez originally introduced the Safe Schools Improvement Act to the House of Representatives in 2007 in order to address the ongoing problem of bullying and harassment in schools. She has worked tirelessly since then to get this bipartisan bill passed. In June 2015, she reintroduced it again to the House along with New York State representative Chris Gibson. It was also introduced to the Senate in January 2015 by Senators Robert Casey (PA) and Mark Kirk (IL). Though the bill has a broad range of support—including the support of 85 percent of Americans, who believe legislation should pass at the federal level to stop bullying in schools—it has yet to receive the support it needs to get to the floor. For my part, I am committed to continuing my efforts to bring awareness to the Safe Schools Improvement Act and to the problem of bullying in schools in hopes that meaningful legislation will pass someday soon to address this very real problem.

Sometimes, though, I wonder whether the problem of bullying comes down to basic human nature. Maybe there are just potential bullies and potential victims, and that will never change.

I'm certainly not trying to pretend I never have mean thoughts about anyone. I'm no saint! I've told people off in my mind, plenty of times. But I have a filter in place that bullies don't have, and that comes down to the simple fact that I would feel so guilty and embarrassed if I said something mean that hurt someone's feelings. Even if I felt vindicated in the moment, five seconds later, I would deeply regret it.

Many people feel that same guilt and regret after hurting someone's feelings. Maybe the problem is just that too many people speak without thinking and regret it later—and it can be so hard to admit when we've done something wrong and apologize. It's all too easy for our egos to get in the way, preventing us from doing what's right.

In 2014, Jason Collins became the first gay pro basketball player to come out publicly. *Time* magazine and several other major news outlets featured him for his bravery. I thought his story was incredibly inspiring, and he has been a big supporter of mine for some time. I was lucky enough to meet him at a screening of my documentary film on the Paramount lot in California, and the picture of us next to each other is so funny. Next to him, I look even tinier than usual. He's about the tallest human being I've ever met!

The next day, he Tweeted the photo of us together, tagged me in it, and included a really sweet caption about meeting me. Inevitably, someone Tweeted back, "What is that horrendous thing standing next to you?"

I just let it go, which is what I sometimes do. It's not necessarily the best way to handle it—ignoring it when someone says something hateful—but there are lots of days when I just don't want to deal with it.

But then I wondered, *What is Jason going to say?* My first thought was that he would probably delete the comment, which is what I would have done, so I was surprised when he actually responded to it directly.

He might have wanted to respond in an aggressive way, but he didn't do that. Instead, his response was, "She's a human being who is inspirational, and maybe you should think about your words before you say them, without knowing the person."

I admire that so much. Not a lot of people would do that. And this is just a guess, but considering his life and his struggles, I imagine Jason Collins has dealt with his fair share of bullying. Even if he hasn't dealt with that on a personal level, he is aware that bullying is a problem, and he is sticking up for people who are smaller and weaker than himself. He is being the change he wishes to see in the world.

That is what I am trying to do. And that is what I am urging you to do, too.

CHAPTER 3

Building Resilience

Over the years, I have told my story again and again, online and in person, to audiences large and small. Over time, I have come to learn that one of the things people are fond of about my story is that it is an example of how resilient we can all be.

I'm not always in touch with that truth, however. Sometimes when I'm hired to get up in front of an audience and tell my life story, it's hard not to wonder how that helps anyone. What does hearing *my* story do for someone else?

I'm all too conscious of the fact that other people may not view my story as universal. They might think I'm unique in some way or that I have some special quality they don't have and couldn't possibly develop. People often ask me how I've overcome so many obstacles—significant health issues, a syndrome that took twenty-five years and countless medical specialists to finally diagnose, and extreme bullying throughout my life. They wonder how I've gotten this far with my kindness and sense of humor intact.

It certainly hasn't been a direct or easy path. But if you ask me, my story isn't really all that unique. Growing up and finding your path is rarely easy for anyone. Everyone struggles with figuring out their values and identities and becoming who they are. That's just part of being human.

Resilience is essential in life, but it doesn't come easily. It's a strength and a skill that has to be developed over time.

It's hard for me to view my life objectively, since I am at the center of my own story. But when I'm able to look at it through an objective lens, I don't see my story as one of struggle or victimization. I see it as a story of resilience, and I tell it because not everyone can tell their own.

Since I have a platform that not everyone has, I can make my voice heard. Therefore, I consider it not just my work but also my calling, my responsibility, and my purpose to speak out and reach as many people as I can with my message that we must be kind to each other, no matter what. We are all in this together. We are all the same.

For a long time, I was like any kid, going through my life and dealing with friends, family, church, and school as they came, on a day-to-day basis. I had my health issues, but it wasn't all difficult, not by a long shot. People around the world now know about the "World's Ugliest Woman" video but that didn't happen until I was in high school.

Before that, my life had fallen into a rhythm, and things were actually going pretty well. Despite the bullying I'd experienced throughout elementary school, I had reached a really good place by middle and early high school.

From kindergarten through fifth grade, I didn't attend my

neighborhood school. Instead, I went to a different school in the district, where my father was a first-grade bilingual teacher. But when I entered sixth grade, my parents enrolled me at the local public middle school near our house. I didn't know anyone there except one friend from church, Rebecca. But that was enough: Having that one friend there with me made all the difference.

Starting at a brand-new school could have been really scary, but I had a lot of confidence. I felt like, *I can do this. It's going to be just fine.* I wasn't nervous at all. Before the school year started, I toured the campus, and walking down those halls with all the other kids who would be brand-new to middle school, just like me, I just felt like...*I got this.*

That was very different for me, going into something new with that much confidence. Making friends happened so naturally, though. Rebecca had always been a loud person, and everyone knew her at our school. People were drawn to us— the loud girl and her quiet friend. With Rebecca as my friend, it was easy to make another friend, Abigail. In turn, Abigail brought her friend Karina into our group, and Karina brought her friend Patsy. Suddenly, the five of us were inseparable.

As I said, I'd always been the quiet one, until Abigail came along. She was quiet, too. It was like we were the same person! We were at the same level, and we just clicked. The five of us all just clicked, actually. Karina was loud like Rebecca, and ditzy—she was so funny. She and Patsy were both native Spanish speakers. Karina spoke English with an accent, which made us laugh. Patsy's English was really good, and she was really, really smart.

We were together all the time. Our parents were friends,

and they shared similar values in how they raised us. Our families would get together on the weekends, and during the week, Rebecca, Abigail, Karina, Patsy, and I were together all day at school. Then, as soon as we got home, we'd be on the phone all evening, just talking about nothing and laughing together. Having those friends come over is one of my favorite memories ever. They really liked to pick on my mom, especially Karina and Patsy. We would lie on my parents' bed and just talk and laugh together.

My friendship with those girls really helped to shape me, and we're still friends to this day. I'm even the godmother of Rebecca's son. Abigail and I have stayed especially close, although the five of us kind of drifted apart after high school. I was the only one who left Austin for college, when I went to Texas State. Now, a decade after high school graduation, when I get together with those friends, it's as if no time has passed. We make fun of each other just like we did when we were young.

I remember in high school, I had to have my appendix out and then have another surgery after that. I ended up needing to be homeschooled for a little while, but my friends would still come over almost every day after school. My mom would make us brownies and popcorn, and my friends would force me to get out of bed. They did not let me feel sorry for myself. They would catch me up on all the gossip and make me laugh and make me feel like I hadn't missed anything. They're still that way to this day. I'm so lucky to have them!

In middle school, I was desperate to join something. At first, I wanted to join band, but I couldn't read the music very well, so everyone talked me out of it. Then Rebecca and I decided to try out for cheerleading together. And we both made it!

Looking back, I can see how crazy it was for me, of all people, to go out for cheerleading. I mean, I'd been excused from PE class my entire life because my body couldn't take it. Even now, I have to be really careful about physical activity, since it's very easy for me to get dehydrated when I sweat. I have no idea why I was so driven to be a cheerleader, except that Rebecca was a gymnast, and there were times when I would go watch her at gymnastics classes after school. It just looked so fun! I wanted to do something fun, too, and felt determined not to let any health issue stop me.

Somehow, despite my tight joints and the ever-present possibility of dehydration, cheerleading turned out to be something I was able to do. Not that it was easy—it was painful! There were some days when I was so sore that I couldn't even walk. But my coach and I figured out how we could modify it in ways that made it easier for me. I didn't have to run when the others did, which was a relief, especially on hot days. Of course, sitting out made me feel like I wasn't one of the group.

So I would push myself. I wanted to work as hard and do as well as everyone else. And I would get dehydrated. That was a big issue during cheerleading; there were plenty of times when I would have to go straight from cheerleading practice to the doctor's office for IV fluids.

My parents were worried about me cheerleading, of course, but once they saw how excited I was about it, they got really excited, too. My mom was terrified, of course. I wanted to try everything, and I didn't care if I got hurt! I wanted to be the one who got tossed up in the air. I was actually the one my coach would experiment with. He would walk around holding me up in the air with one hand.

Once my team got over thinking they might break me, cheerleading was really fun. But when I watch videos my mom took of me cheerleading at home games, I just laugh. The picture is so shaky, and you can hardly hear our cheers over the sound of my mom's anxious chanting—"Don't fall, don't fall, *don't fall!*"

It was pretty amazing that my parents supported me in doing that. There were so many risks. If they'd said no and tried to prevent me from doing it, though, it would have been a huge fight. I was stubborn back then, even more so than I am now. Thank goodness my mom and dad saw the benefits of my joining the group, and that outweighed the risks, for them and for me.

My friends supported me, too. Karina, Patsy, and Abigail would come to the games and sit right in front, and it was like they were my cheerleaders. It was the best!

I kept going with cheerleading in high school, but Rebecca didn't. When you're in middle school, your interests seem to change almost every day, and the five of us were always into something different. We accepted each other as individuals, and while we had our differences from time to time, we were always able to stick together as a group.

Even now, it's around those four friends that I am able to be the most open and vulnerable. I've always been able to tell them exactly how I'm feeling in the moment, about anything at all. When we were seniors and Patsy and Karina started dating boys, they would talk about it when we hung out. I was able to be honest with them and tell them, "I'm so happy for you, but if I seem quiet, it's because I wish I could have those experiences, too."

That was tough for me to admit. I push myself to put on a bright, strong face, even when I'm experiencing anxiety or doubts about myself. Feeling comfortable enough to talk openly and honestly with my friends about anything that might come up, and to have them support me, without making me feel embarrassed—that was really meaningful for me growing up.

Aside from my family, my relationship with those four girls is the secret to my resilience.

Support systems are everything. They can make all the difference in the world, especially when it comes to building inner strength that stands the test of time. It's easier to bounce back from tough emotions and experiences when you know there's at least one person who has your back. As the saying goes, *No man is an island.* In my toughest moments, it was my inner circle that would pick me up and dust off my bruises so I could keep going. If negative thoughts take over my mind, my friends remind me again of who I truly am.

So what I want people to know is, I don't have superhuman strength because of my experiences, but if I were a superwoman, my friends and family would be that magical potion that kept me going. I have found that most people who are known for being strong or resilient have similar people in their lives.

———

Having good friendships makes you stronger and a better person. It's never too late to make good friendships or reconnect with old ones. My family and friends have been a huge influence in shaping the person I have become. They have not only helped me stand up again after setbacks, but best of all, they are there for me in the good times, too. Everyone needs friends like that, friends who will always be there no matter what.

Abigail and I still talk frequently. While I don't get to connect as often with Rebecca, Karina, or Patsy, whenever we do, it's as if no time has passed at all. We pick up right where we left off, and that makes me happy!

When my documentary came out in theaters, there was a day when I was just dead from all the publicity and traveling I'd been doing. Karina and Patsy sent me Snapchats that day as they went to see the movie. It made me feel so good! They sent me pictures of themselves in the car on the way, and buying their tickets, and posing by the movie poster. They were really surprised when they watched the film. Before that, I don't think they really knew what I did for a living! They just knew I was gone all the time.

To know they had seen the film and to hear them say, "That's exactly how we know you; that was *you* on the screen," I was *really* pleased.

They have been an essential part of the building blocks of my resilience. And their friendship has taught me as much as my family has about the importance of kindness.

Just like the path toward kindness, the path toward resilience can be a bumpy one. But with a good support system, anyone can feel better about themselves—and that can lead to feeling better about the world as a whole.

I like to think I've done a good job of being selective about the friends I've chosen to let into my personal life, but that isn't necessarily true. Some angels have come my way purely through the grace of God.

Not all my closest friendships have been as simple as the ones I share with my five middle-school girlfriends. Sometimes I've allowed people into my heart who ended up causing real drama in my life. But even difficult relationships or experiences are gifts, and we should be grateful for them. I'm grateful for the disagreements and other painful moments, because springing back has made me even stronger.

CHAPTER 4

Are They or Aren't They?

The notion of love for self, family, friends, and community is wonderful and a huge part of this book, but as humans, we'd be ill prepared as a culture if we did not acknowledge our innate desire to be loved by a significant other. Personal relationships are often the most challenging and rewarding aspects of our lives. I don't mean the relationships that we inherit—such as from our children and family members—but those we attract, the boyfriends, the wives, and all the in-betweens. My point is, the more we can accept and embrace our innate desire to feel loved by a significant other, the kinder the world will be.

It doesn't mean that everyone will find their soul mate right away, but it is important that we appreciate this aspect of our biological makeup. If not, things can get sticky; people become unhappy and lonely, they experience feelings of isolation and lack of hope and, ultimately, become prone to do mean things. (Remember, hurt people hurt people.)

I am the first to admit that the whole "finding love" journey can be a rough one. The truth is, no one is perfect, yet we're all afraid at some point that the person we love may notice that we are not. When hearts are involved, our insecurities come into play—those tender spots we all have that, when pressed on or bumped up against, flare to life. It's easy to slip into the mind-set that our flaws make us unlovable. That's why we try to show only our best sides, our best selves, on dating apps and first dates, when we're just getting to know someone new who could turn out to be special. We hide the weaker, messier parts of ourselves, the parts we aren't so proud of, because somewhere deep down, we believe we don't deserve love if we aren't perfect.

I've definitely gotten caught up in that way of thinking. I've dated a lot, but for a long time, I was very critical of myself. My insecurities about my appearance and everything else really used to get in the way of my love life. It's hard to connect with someone when you can't believe they could ever like you or be attracted to you! Unfortunately, that's just the kind of mind-set I used to have.

I'm often asked about my love life but I'm not too surprised because it's an important subject! For a long time, I joked that it seemed like my romantic status must be the only interesting thing about me. Every time I gave an interview, they would never fail to ask, "So, do you have a boyfriend?" Fans frequently ask me the same question, along with people who follow me on social media. Now it's time to lay any and all rumors to rest. Here it is, the information you've all been waiting for—the truth about my romantic status. Drum roll, please!

Currently, I am...

Wait for it...

Still searching for my *person*—that special guy who will be my one and only, forever. Whether I find him or not may be irrelevant; it's more important that I value myself enough to know it's possible.

Whenever I was asked about my romantic status by an interviewer or a fan, I'd always brush the question aside. Of course, when I would post a picture on social media of myself with someone I was dating, I was well aware of the irony that it probably appeared I had a lot going on in that department. People who didn't know me might think I was happy to be dating casually, without realizing I had that yearning, that constant wish to find true love.

No matter what an interviewer or a fan might ask me, I would always try to phrase my answer in the best possible light. I thought I couldn't live up to my job of being brave and positive if I revealed my true reality. The truth was, after too many near misses in my love life, I often struggled with loneliness, and my romantic status was complicated at best. While I've gotten serious with a few guys I've dated, I've still never had an official boyfriend.

Case in point: my relationship with Blake.

(Note: I'm changing certain people's names out of respect for their privacy!)

Blake was the first friend I made as a freshman at Texas State. We met on our second or third day on campus, as we both stood waiting for an elevator. I was holding a bag of textbooks with the word BOOKSTORE printed across it in huge letters. It was just the two of us waiting, and for the first minute, we stood there in silence.

Then Blake spoke. "Were you just at the bookstore?"

I remember thinking, *Well, yeah—it's on the bag!* But I didn't say that, of course. We made small talk. He asked my name and I told him, and that was it. I didn't think anything of it.

The next day, I ran into him on the elevator again.

"Hey, Lacie!" he greeted me.

I stared at him and then laughed. "Lacie? That's not my name!"

After that, he would call me Lacie whenever he wanted to make me giggle. It became one of many running jokes between us.

Blake ran for president of our dorm that semester, and he won. Everyone loved him. He was very charismatic, a big people person. He would talk to anyone who had a pulse and become their friend. He happened to live one floor below me in the room directly under mine, and we'd become friends on Myspace. I was doing speaking engagements at the time, and he was taking a speech class, so one day he asked if I would come downstairs to the study room to hear his speech.

He told me it would be with a group of people, but it turned out it was just me! I kept thinking more people would be coming, but five minutes into his speech, no one else had shown up. Finally, he admitted he'd only invited me.

Little did I know at the time, we would develop a long, life-changing friendship.

For two years, we both lived on campus, until I had to

go home to Austin for surgery. When I recovered and went back to school, Blake and I decided to get a place together off campus, so we were housemates during our junior and senior years. But there were many aspects to our relationship that made us much more than just friends or roommates.

Blake was really good both to me and for me. There were times when it was *so* good between us—when it was perfect. We were alike in many ways, and it was very easy to be around him. Our conversations flowed, and we always seemed to be on the same page.

Our relationship may have started out as a chance encounter at an elevator, but over time, Blake had become my most immediate and important support system—handsome, hilarious Blake. We were great friends from the start, and slowly, he started to become my everything.

Just a couple of weeks after we met, he took me to his hometown for the first time. I met the friends he'd grown up with, along with his immediate and extended family, and everyone welcomed me with open arms. I felt as if I'd known them forever. My own family embraced Blake just as warmly and completely.

We were so incredibly close for so many years that still, a decade later, I look back on my relationship with him and wonder why things went the way they did. We shared an undeniable chemistry from the very beginning, which blurred the lines of our friendship. Living together blurred them even more, until our mutual friends had no idea whether we were a couple or just best friends—and many times, neither did we.

Every time we posted a picture together on social media, people would leave comments asking, "Are they together or aren't they?" I would never answer those questions, partly because I never exactly knew the answer myself.

Lots of nights, we would spend hours lying together in Blake's bed, just talking about nothing. There were times when we would be quiet, and Blake would hold my hand, and that was it. There would be other times when he would look at me with those big, brown eyes of his and tell me, "You're my *person*. You're perfect for me."

How could I not fall in love with him? The only problem, of course, was that we weren't a couple. There was something very intense between us, but whatever that was, we never defined it. Blake dated other people off and on throughout our relationship, which was always so difficult for me to accept.

We met at a point in our lives when we were both struggling to find ourselves. We were young, just emerging from the cocoons of our families and our childhoods, and poised at the edge of independence, adulthood, and responsibility. In some very important ways, Blake and I grew up together—and it was a fast and furious ride. The friendship we forged allowed us both to become very clear on who we were as individuals and who we wanted to become. That's the power of love! We learned an incredible amount from each other, which is why I've come to appreciate the importance of finding your *person*. It's not only about the results and expectations but also the process of learning that you deserve to be loved is just as important.

Blake and I are still in touch, here and there. We aren't completely out of each other's lives, and we do reach out to one another every once in a while. Every time we do, it's the same as it always was. I still feel that inexorable pull, that attraction that connects us. I don't think that will ever go away. The truth is, I don't want it to.

To this day, I still go through periods when Blake is on my mind constantly, especially when I'm dealing with health issues. He was my rock, my strong shoulder to lean on when I was filled with anxiety about what might lie ahead. He took me to doctors' appointments and sat with me in emergency rooms when I needed him. To this day, he is still the only person in my life outside my family who has ever done that for me. I loved him for it, and I still do. I really do.

One night not too long ago, I had a lot on my mind. I'd just gone through one surgery, and I had another coming up. All the old anxieties were surfacing, and I wanted to talk to Blake.

Late that night, I texted him: "Are you up?"

Almost instantly, he responded: "What's wrong? I can tell something is wrong."

He knew. Somehow, he knew from that simple text that I needed him. The deep bond was still there between us. I will always love him for giving me that feeling. Everyone on the planet deserves that feeling. The feeling of knowing that someone is there for you and it's not because anyone told them to be. It's just because they love you.

Even though Blake and I were never officially a couple, I consider him my first love.

––––––––

At twenty-eight, I have observed that love relationships and marriages are now underrated in our culture. But they shouldn't be! Let's be honest, love is one of our most common interests. What I want for my future is a lot like what my parents have built together. They have been married nearly thirty years, and they act like they're still dating. That's what I want, too! I want a family of my own, a house of my own, and a relationship with a guy who loves me for me.

Of course, I can't have a relationship that's exactly like my parents', since I didn't meet my true love in high school. My parents met when they were still in high school, and they've been together ever since.

They met at a dance in the tiny town of Gonzales, Texas, where my mother grew up. My dad asked her to dance, but they only got to spend a few minutes together because my grandpa, Popo, was incredibly strict. They hardly even managed to exchange names before Popo drove up and yelled at my mom to get into the car. Whenever my parents tell that story, it reminds me of the clock striking midnight and Cinderella having to dash back to her coach before it turns into a pumpkin.

Somehow, both my parents knew they'd made a connection, and they both knew that nothing—not their young ages, not their strict parents, and certainly not the fact that they had no idea how to find each other again—would keep them apart.

That night, my mom told her best friend she'd met the boy she was going to marry someday. That same night, my dad told his mother about my mom. He said, "I don't know anything about her, or how I'm going to find her again. All I know is that her name is Rita, she has incredible hazel eyes, and I'm going to marry her."

He knew. They both knew.

My dad lived in Waelder, a small town near Gonzales,

so he got a job at a restaurant in Gonzales in hopes that he would run into my mom again. When I think about a guy doing that, it sounds so stalkerish! (Sorry, Dad!) He wasn't a stalker, of course—he just knew my mom was *it* for him. It's so incredible that they both knew with such certainty that they were meant to be together, based on nothing more than a brief encounter at a high school dance. Their small-town, modern-day Cinderella story gives me shivers in the best way. It definitely seems their love was meant to be.

In case you're wondering, my dad's restaurant job scheme worked. He got the job, they found each other again, and after four years of dating, they married. They've been together ever since.

Their love was meant to be, and I was their first child—the first product of their love. I firmly believe they were meant to be my parents. They're so good together, and so good to and for me. They've taught me so much about how to handle this crazy, unpredictable life, and they've given me a beautifully realistic view of what it looks like to love someone enough to make it work, to help each other through the rough times, no matter what comes up.

They've also shown me how to keep laughing, even when life gets tough. I love the way my dad can always bring things back into perspective, no matter what's going on. I want to marry a guy like that someday—a man who can remind me that whatever it is, it's not that serious, and no matter how bad it seems, things could be a lot worse. Everyone deserves that kind of love from someone and should aspire to be that kind of love for someone else.

———

A couple of years ago, I fell hard and fast all over again when I met Kyle, a handsome, inspiring helicopter pilot whom I dated for the better part of a year. Kyle and I took it really slowly at first, even though I was incredibly attracted to him from the start. He was sweet, but as always, it was hard to tell what he really thought about me at first or what his agenda was.

You see, dating isn't as straightforward for me as it is for most people my age. When I meet someone, whether in person or online, I always have to wonder, *What's their real motive?* That sounds terrible, but it's true. I've been on a few different dating apps, and it's always obvious from my profile pictures that, while I may have great hair and a bright smile, my looks are a bit unique. When a new match notification pops up on my dating app, it's hard not to wonder what this new person's real intentions might be.

This concern probably says more about me and my own insecurities than it does about the guys I've dated. For a long time, in the back of my mind, I wondered if my insecurities about my appearance might be the real reason I didn't have a boyfriend. How could I expect a guy to be attracted to me if I wasn't fully confident in myself, including my looks? That was my secret conviction: No guy could possibly be attracted to me, and no matter who I met or started crushing on, I would always be stuck in the friend zone. Part of me was convinced I wouldn't be ready to start thinking more seriously about dating until I could get to the point where I felt confident about every aspect of myself.

That wasn't true, of course, and it wasn't a kind way to treat myself. I know that now: People don't need to be perfectly strong and confident in order to form fulfilling relationships. I also know that I am not alone in that sort of thinking; many of us feel like there might be some handicap that is keeping us single or from being loved. People come up with all types of creative reasons why they don't deserve love: They're too fat, too skinny, too old, too poor, too plain, too sexy, and the list goes on and on. We have these self-loathing narratives on autoplay, and we constantly beat ourselves up with them, but they are not true. False reasoning should not hold you back from pursuing a serious connection.

Kyle and I met through a dating app, so our profile pictures were the first thing we saw about each other. I thought he was cute, but I had no idea what he thought of me on that level. That made me nervous. It also made me nervous not to know how much he knew, or *thought* he knew, about me, my work, and my life.

That's another thing that makes dating tricky for me: There's a good chance that any guy looking at my profile already knows who I am and at least a little bit of my story. That's why, when a new guy contacts me, I want to know right away how much he knows about my life. In a way, it's easier to date guys who have no idea who I am. With no preconceptions, there's a clean slate between us.

I was thankful to find out that Kyle knew nothing about my public persona. That made it so much more real and exciting to get to know each other. Several times, he said he felt bad that he didn't know more about me or my work, but every time he mentioned it, I assured him it was a good thing. It was *so* good! It meant he was just getting to know me for me.

Once, when we were out on a date, a group of teenage girls approached us and were so excited to meet me that Kyle said, "I really don't know what I'm getting into, do I?"

My answer was perfectly honest: "No, you really don't!"

But then, neither did I. Does anyone really know what they're getting into, in the heady rush of a brand-new romance? That's what it's all about—peeling back the layers and discovering who this new person really is on the inside and whether they might be the right one for you. For some of us, our hesitance to try on some real love is solely based on fear.

The issue of what he thought about my looks was on my mind heavily from the very start, until finally, a week or two into our relationship, I worked up the courage to address it directly. His response was absolutely perfect.

It should have been obvious from the beginning that he liked the way I looked. He was always giving me random, spontaneous compliments about my smile or my eyes. Still, it was hard for me to believe. Could he truly not care that my appearance was different from other women?

The first time we FaceTimed, I was so nervous that my hand was shaking as I held my phone. But we ended up talking for two hours, and it was wonderful.

That helped me become bold enough to address the elephant in the room. We hadn't even had our first date yet but I desperately needed to know that if we got involved, our relationship would unfold on an even playing field.

One day I texted him: "Are you talking to me because you feel sorry for me or you pity me?"

His answer to that extremely vulnerable question was so powerful. I still remember the exact words he texted back to me—I don't think I'll ever forget them.

"Why would I pity you?" he wrote. "You're a young, vibrant woman with the world at her fingertips. I don't see anything to pity there."

That text meant everything to me. *Was it possible that it had not occurred to him?* I thought. And then he sent another: "I don't feel sorry for you. You did your best with the hand you were dealt. That takes spunk, tenacity, and drive. That's why I love talking to you—you always have a great day."

Now, don't get me wrong: I definitely *don't* always have a great day. No one is happy every day, including me—far from it, in fact. But Kyle's response was so meaningful to me that at first, I couldn't even reply. I couldn't have formed a coherent thought if I'd tried; all I could do was take in his words for a moment and simply appreciate them. He'd expressed exactly what I believed on my best days, but what was all too easy for me to forget on the bad ones.

Still, many realizations about myself came to light early in our relationship. I've always been the type to want to help other people; I always try to do whatever they need to feel special and loved. Having someone like Kyle in my life, someone who wanted to make *me* feel special for no other reason than my own happiness, was a new experience for me. It was something I'd always dreamed of, but now that I was finally experiencing it firsthand, I was starting to realize it wasn't as easy to accept as I thought. I had always been in charge of my own happiness. Suddenly, it was time to let someone else make me happy, and it was a struggle for me to realize that was okay.

My relationship with Kyle was incredibly meaningful to me, and the feelings we shared were true and real. But we were two different people on two different paths in life. Although it felt perfect, if there's one thing I've learned over the years, it's that things are never quite how they appear from the outside.

A few years ago, before I ever met Kyle, my whole extended family attended the *quinceañera* (a Sweet Fifteen party) of one of my younger cousins. At the reception, I sat at a table with Marina, Chris, and our parents. My cousin Nikki sat at the next table over with her son, her boyfriend, and her parents, and at the table just beyond that sat my other cousin Anna and her parents, along with her boyfriend and her son. Growing up, Nikki, Anna, and I always hit all our milestones together—going to middle school, then high school, having our *quinceañeras*, graduating high school, and going on to college…everything!

I remember sitting there, looking at my cousins and their families, thinking, *Why don't I have that?* We'd always hit our life milestones together. I caught myself staring at them and feeling wistful.

Later in the evening, Nikki brought me a margarita, and we ended up sitting together and half yelling to each other over the noise of the party. Nikki is a volleyball coach now, and she loves her job. Still, she was telling me, "You get to do so many cool things. You get to travel all over the place, and your life is so easy! It's so great that you're having so many fun experiences."

That was so ironic to hear. I told her I'd just been having the exact same thoughts about her life. "I've been looking at you and Anna and your families," I said, "just wishing I had what you have. You're so lucky."

"It's not easy," she said. "It's not necessarily how it looks from the outside." She told me about some issues she'd had—difficulties with work and parenting, things I hadn't even considered, looking from the outside in. I mean, she and her little family looked so happy together. But she said that wasn't an exact reflection of her reality.

"Then you get it," I told her. "Because what you see of my life isn't necessarily my reality, either."

It was eye-opening to have that conversation with her—to know someone else was thinking the same things about me, right when I'd been thinking them about her. It was definitely a grass-is-always-greener type of situation. It was also a lesson in realizing that everyone has both blessings and challenges.

This is an important thing to remember, each and every day. When you're feeling a little down, a little less loved, or a tad more lonely, and you see someone who seems to have it all, it's so easy to slip into envy over whatever you think they have that you don't. The truth is, you have no idea. They might even be looking at you and feeling envious of something they think you have that they lack!

I am grateful for my relationship with Kyle because it helped me learn the truth of that, not just in my head, but also in my heart: that I deserve unconditional acceptance in a relationship and that attraction can exist both in spite of my appearance and because of it. I'll never forget that incredible lesson in love. Kyle helped me internalize it to the point that I could actually start believing it about myself.

That is true for all of us. If you ever slip into thinking you have to be perfect to deserve love, remind yourself that *no one* is perfect, and *everyone* deserves love. We all deserve love, acceptance, and respect. Furthermore, although I believe more love will make our culture stronger and that none of it should be spared, being in a relationship isn't the only important thing in life! You don't need to be in a romantic relationship to feel confident or whole. You can be single and still know you're worthy of love. You're good enough as you are. You're beautiful as you are! But equally accept that it is natural for everyone to love and be loved. We don't need to run from love; we need to run toward it.

CHAPTER 5

How Do You Define Yourself?

How we define ourselves is critical. Making the decision not to let anyone else define us and then choosing how to define ourselves and what we're all about—these are essential steps in life for each of us. And they have everything to do with moving forward on a path toward kindness.

Defining ourselves in a conscious way is an act of self-empowerment. Current events make doing so more important than ever before in how we use that power to create a better world. In 2016, when many details came out in the media about a high-profile Stanford rape case, "Be the Swede" memes started popping up all over social media. These referred to the two Stanford grad students, both Swedish, who had discovered the attack in progress and saved the victim from further harm.

Those "Be the Swede" memes reminded me of a story about

Fred Rogers, the beloved host of the classic children's TV show *Mister Rogers' Neighborhood.* When Mr. Rogers was a little boy and he would see scary things on the news, his mother would tell him, "Look for the helpers. You will always find people who are helping."

That message is so meaningful to me. For decades, Mr. Rogers taught lessons in kindness and friendship to the millions of children who watched his program, and that message— *Look for the helpers*—speaks to why. For Mr. Rogers, kindness started at home, with a mother who was wise enough to teach him that as much evil as there is in the world, there is even more goodness.

All too often, we hear stories about bad things that happened because people didn't get involved when they should have. Accidents and even tragedies can occur when no one is willing to stand up or step forward, yet we make all kinds of excuses as to why getting involved is difficult, inappropriate, or even impossible.

I get it. It's so easy to become hardened to others' misfortune. Anyone who's lived or worked in an urban area has probably walked past homeless people countless times, avoiding their gaze because it's easier to look away than to try to help.

But helping others is essential. I want to take that message, *Look for the helpers*, one step further. When something bad happens or tragedy strikes, instead of just looking for the helpers, I urge you to *be* the helper. I urge you to define yourself right now as a kind person—as a helper. That way, when something terrible happens, when someone is struggling or you witness an injustice, you won't be so quick to turn away.

Instead, you might decide to be the Swede—to be the helper, the person who stands up, steps forward, and gets involved.

How do you define yourself? However *else* you define yourself—and there are a million different, wonderful ways— I hope you will consider also defining yourself as a helper. I hope you will define yourself as someone who is kind to yourself and to others.

Be the helper. Be the kindness that you wish to see in the world.

———

Ever since the TEDx AustinWomen talk I gave in 2013 entitled "How Do You Define Yourself?" my career has really taken off. I didn't know at the time how much that talk's message would come to mean to me. Its title alone encapsulates something that is pivotal to me, in various ways, personally and in my career.

It took me a long time to reach the point where I could define myself as a speaker. It all started back in high school, when I was an office aide for the assistant principal of my school. A day was coming up when half the grades would be in testing, so the school was planning to hold two different assemblies for the grades that weren't testing. The assistant principal asked me to speak at the assemblies and just tell my story.

I still don't know why she asked me to do that! Initially, I turned her invitation down. I mean, tell my story? I didn't even know that was a *thing*. I'd never heard of that—just going up in front of a bunch of people and talking about your life.

But she asked me to discuss it with my parents and consider it, so I did. My friends really encouraged me to do it.

Finally, I agreed. I wrote down my speech word for word, printed it out, and put it in a folder. When the day came, I went up onstage and I read my speech.

Fortunately, it ended up going really well. The principal had warned me not to feel bad if the audience got kind of loud. They were ninth graders, after all. That warning was a little nerve-wracking, but while I was talking, I realized everyone in the audience was being really quiet and respectful. At one point I looked up, and it dawned on me that they were absolutely intent on what I was saying. They were leaning forward and giving me 100 percent of their attention.

I put my folder down and just started talking to them. It went so well—and it came so naturally, which was a huge surprise.

That experience lit a fire inside me. I kept wanting to relive the experience so I could feel that way again. I kept thinking, *How can I do this again?* So I went home and researched how to become a speaker. My primary tool? YouTube!

It's ironic to me now that YouTube, of all things, was my first and biggest tool in learning to be a motivational speaker. I mean, really, YouTube has been a huge part of my life and my development, both personal and professional. It's been both my nemesis and my best friend. I used it to educate myself on motivational speakers. Coincidentally, a year or so later, I discovered the "World's Ugliest Woman" video on YouTube, which was so incredibly hurtful but ended up honing my life's work in an incredible way. After that, I started my own YouTube channel to post videos, spread my message of positivity, and reach my many thousands of followers. I still post videos there to this day. The truth is, I can't live without YouTube!

Back when I first used it as a tool to learn about speaking in front of an audience, I watched video after video of different speakers—mostly Bill Rancic at first. For some reason, he was the first person who popped up in my search, so he became the focal point of my research. I studied his website, I studied what his website was, and of course I watched a ton of videos of him speaking. I took notes about his methods: Did he use note cards, a PowerPoint, or a video? Did he walk around while he talked? Did he sit down or stand behind a podium? I tried each of those different options and techniques myself, experimenting with them in my own speeches to figure out what worked best for me.

I never practiced by myself in my room or even in front of my family. I wanted real, firsthand practice, in front of an audience of strangers. So I Googled all kinds of local places, contacted them, and said, "If you need a speaker, I'm available." In the very beginning, of course, I'd only done those two speeches at my school. That was all that was on my résumé, if you could even call it a résumé at that point—but I didn't tell them that!

On the weekends, I would go speak. It started out with churches that would invite me to speak to their congregations. Back then, of course, I did it all for free, because I needed the experience. Over time, I tried everything at least once: PowerPoints, videos, everything.

Nowadays, I don't use any of that; I just talk.

I'm glad my identity shifted and expanded to include that role. When it comes to following your passion, it's essential to see yourself as whatever it is that you're trying to become. If you can't envision yourself in your new identity—as a painter, for example, or a new student, or in a new job—who else is going to take you seriously in that role? I do know how hard that can be, though, especially when you're first starting out on your path. Whatever goal you're pursuing, if it's truly your passion, that means the emotional stakes are incredibly high.

And putting yourself out there, in whatever way that applies to you, is tough. It's so easy to overthink it. As soon as you put it out in front of other people, if you're anything like me, self-doubt and anxiety start crowding in. Suddenly, all you can see is what's wrong with what you made and where it needs improvement. It's hard to see anything good about it.

Sound familiar? We are all our own worst critics. No one else is going to pick out the little flaws that we can spot so easily in our own lives. That's not what anyone else is tuned in to.

There is something I've learned through my work as a motivational speaker: When people come to see me speak, they're attending my talk in order to have an emotional experience, and one that I hope is transformative for them. They want to leave the auditorium feeling inspired—feeling as if they have reached a higher emotional level than the one they were on when they walked in.

All the nitpicky stuff—the flaws and mistakes I can pick out in my work, the little things I might wish I had said or done differently? Most of the time, those don't matter nearly as much as I thought. I believe this is a general truth for all of us: What matters is the heart and intention behind what you do. Positive intentions will shine through it all.

Connecting with and inspiring people: That has been my passion since I was a young teenager. I remember a certain photo of Bill Rancic that always stood out to me. In it, he's standing in the middle of a huge arena surrounded by hundreds, maybe even thousands, of people. I used to look at that photo in high school, and I would tell myself, *I'll know I've made it when I speak to that many people.* Fast-forward to the fall of 2014, when I spoke onstage for the Fundación Telmex Siglo XXI event in Mexico City. Hillary Clinton and Mark Zuckerberg were speakers at the same event—and we were all speaking in front of ten thousand people! All I kept thinking about that day was that photo and the fact that I'd done it. *I did it!*

After that, I mentioned Bill Rancic enough times in interviews that his people ended up reaching out to me. I even got to have lunch with him! I was freaking out—*freaking out!* I went with Sara, and we met with Bill and his manager at the time, whose name was John and who has since become one of our biggest supporters. He worked at E! News, and he did everything he could to help us with our Kickstarter campaign when we started making the documentary.

We met Bill and John at Barney's in Los Angeles. I was so nervous and excited—too excited to eat! I ordered ice cream, because I was too keyed up for real food, but we ended up talking like old friends. Bill was so nice and down to earth. He gave me a lot of advice to consider when thinking about what I wanted my speaking career to look like. He told me that it's okay to say no sometimes, which was really important for me to take in. Like lots of people, I can have a tough time saying no. But pushing myself too far can take a real toll on my health, and very quickly. As soon as he said it, I knew it was a lesson I needed to learn.

Bill even gave me financial advice. He said, "I tell my wife this all the time: When you're making money, you can't just go around spending it. You have to save it, because it could all be gone tomorrow."

It was such a wonderful, full-circle moment to be able to tell him in person, "I studied you. And now here I am with you, telling you about *my* speaking career!" It was crazy, in the best possible way.

When he gave me his cell phone number, I almost died. I've never used it, of course. I mean, if I called or texted him, I don't even know what in the world I would say. I just feel good having it. Just in case. In case *what*, I have no idea—but it's in my phone, and it's not going anywhere.

I've never met his wife, Giuliana, but at the time that I met Bill, they were busy doing the last season of their reality show together. I really like her! They are one of the few couples in Hollywood that have managed to do a reality show together and not end up getting a divorce. That says a lot about the kind of people they are and the strength of the relationship they've built together.

That's the long version of how I choose to define myself and how it has brought me to where I am today as a motivational speaker.

————

When I first started speaking in front of audiences, my goal was to get into a speakers' bureau. A year ago, I achieved that goal! Of course I see it differently now, but at that point, when I was first launching my career, I saw that as the pinnacle of success. If my career was the marathon I wanted to run, joining a speakers' bureau represented the finish line.

I had several offers from various bureaus over the years, but for a long time, I turned them down. I liked being the one in control. It was tough to stay on top of all the details, but it was work I enjoyed—until there were just so many details, so many invitations and engagements and travel arrangements to make, that it got overwhelming.

In the past, other people who have wanted to represent me have wanted to change what I say in my speeches or improve it in some way according to their own ideas. They've wanted to shape and mold me, to define me to my audiences in whatever way seemed best to them instead of letting me define myself.

When I met my agent, Curt, I could tell he was different. During that lunch with Curt, I told him about my long and winding path toward becoming a motivational speaker. I told him about how I crafted my own speeches, just as I'd done from the very beginning: After I come up with the topic I want to speak about, I write out three bullet points, so that as I'm speaking in front of an audience, I can shape it in my head and know where I want to go with the speech. Overall, I simply trust myself to say whatever comes to me in the moment.

When I explained my speaking style to Curt, he said that's a skill speakers need—to know how to adjust their words and delivery within the first five minutes, so they can change and sculpt their speech in the moment in order to grab the audience.

Then Curt brought up a key point: When you're giving a

speech, he told me, you have to ask yourself, *How can I make my audience the hero?* He said your task is to figure out how to make anyone who's listening the hero of their own story. That resonated with me and that was the intention when I gave the speech "How Do You Define Yourself?" It signified a turning point in my career, but also in my personal agenda.

Recognizing my gift as a speaker to make my audience their own hero and making the conscious decision to include that in how I defined myself to the world—that was a meaningful and empowering step for me as a helper.

———

Deciding how you want to define yourself to the world requires you to take a moment to reflect on your life. Wherever you are right now, you've gotten there because of your own remarkable qualities and experiences. *You* are the person who led the way to where you are today. The good choices you've made and the bad ones, the positive experiences you've had and the negative ones—all of it is your story. No one else has the same story as you, and that's a good thing. If we all had the same story to tell, we would get really sick of hearing it over and over again!

You have your very own recipe for success in life, based on a unique mix of ingredients. Those ingredients are *you*—the qualities that you bring to the table, made up of your own personality and experiences. Your uniqueness is your gift to the world.

Sometimes, other people take what's unique about us and reduce it to a quick, convenient label. *Victim, diva, geek*—all of these are labels sometimes imposed on people that may or may not have anything to do with who they are inside.

We don't have to allow ourselves to be defined by the labels imposed on us. We get to define ourselves.

My syndrome is just a part of me; it doesn't define me. I am who I am both in spite of and because of my syndrome. I'm glad I have it! It took me years to reach a place where I could finally say that, but now I can honestly say, "Yeah, I look a little different. So what?"

People have called me "ugly" and even a "freak" in the past, but I do not identify with those labels, and I don't let them define me. Instead, I choose to define myself. How do I define myself? Oh, in so many, many ways!

One way is as a brave risk-taker: As a middle-school student with a tiny, vulnerable body, I threw myself fearlessly into cheerleading. As a high schooler with no idea of what I was getting myself into, I hung out my shingle and launched my career as a motivational speaker. I'm proud of my ability to step well outside my comfort zone.

I discuss my medical issues in my talks, especially as related to how my identity has changed as my doctors and specialists, along with my family and I, have come to understand exactly what we're dealing with when it comes to my health. I used to define myself as the "Undiagnosed Girl," and what a world-shaking thing it was for me when suddenly, at age twenty-five, I was finally given a diagnosis.

Being the Undiagnosed Girl my whole life had convinced me I was some kind of rarity—and that being a rarity was what was special about me. The Undiagnosed Girl wasn't just how I defined myself; it was my entire identity. It was like my middle name, so much a part of who I was that when I suddenly lost it, I had no idea who I was anymore.

Anyone who watched our documentary got to see that transition in real time. There's a scene in the film where my family and I are at my genetics doctor's office in Houston, when we find out I have neonatal progeroid syndrome, or NPS.

NPS is a combination of Marfan syndrome and lipodystrophy. Lipodystrophy is responsible for my inability to gain weight, while Marfan syndrome is a genetic disorder that affects my vision, my heart, and my body's connective tissue. The form of Marfan syndrome that I have is very rare, and in my particular case, it puts my aortic valve at risk of dangerous dilation. As the valve to the body's main artery, the aortic valve is a biggie, so the risk of it becoming enlarged is a very real and present threat that I live with every day.

All of these details are what I have learned in the three years since receiving my diagnosis. But at first, I didn't fully understand my diagnosis, nor did I understand what it truly meant for my life, my identity, my family, or my future.

If you watched the film, you saw me being strong as we received the diagnosis. Being positive. And I wasn't faking it. At first, I truly felt relieved, like, *Finally. Finally, we know what's wrong with me. Now we can move forward.*

But it wasn't long before I fell into a brutal downward spiral as a direct result of losing the identity—the Undiagnosed Girl—that I hadn't even realized I'd shaped my whole life around.

These days, when I speak in front of an audience, I don't dwell as much as I used to on the medical stuff or on my childhood experiences with bullying. I might talk about my life in that way for a few minutes at most, but then I move on. There is so much more to me that I want to explore and share with people.

In Malaysia, where I spoke in July 2015 at the National Achievers Congress, I was one of two women co-headlining the event. The National Achievers Congress is a major three-day event that has been held for over twenty years now in multiple countries around the world. Hugely famous people speak at their events—household names like Richard Branson. My being included as a speaker was a real honor. And being asked to co-headline? Unbelievable. It was an enormous honor and an equally enormous responsibility.

For my talk, I discussed a subject I'd never spoken about before: being an entrepreneur. At that point, I didn't even think of myself as an entrepreneur! That definitely wasn't yet part of how I defined myself to the world. But I really wanted to give an excellent speech, even more so than usual. I mean, being one of the first two women to headline such a large event—that was big. Plus, we'd traveled so far to get there.

However, I was also really sick. I could hardly breathe! During my speech, I kept telling myself, *Just get through this sentence without coughing, and you're good.* Somehow, it worked. I got through the talk, I connected with my audience, and I was really proud of what I'd accomplished. My health doesn't define me—I define my health and my career. Those definitions keep expanding, and so do I.

CHAPTER 6

The Myth of Positivity

When I talk to people about creating a culture of kindness, sometimes I get the feeling they may think I'm asking for a lot. After all, doesn't that mean we have to be kind and positive *all the time*? But staying kind and positive every second of every day isn't possible! We're human; we aren't perfect. We get tired, we snap, we lash out. It happens. But striving for kindness toward ourselves and others and trying to keep a positive outlook— these are achievable goals, and I believe they are worthy ones.

The instinct to stay positive is one a lot of us have, and it's both a blessing and a curse. Being positive shares plenty of parallels with being kind, and the two qualities overlap in many of us. Think about it: People who are positive smile a lot, look on the bright side of life, and encourage others to do the same. People who are kind tend to smile a lot, too! They want to help and comfort others, which goes hand in hand with a positive attitude. Kind people and positive people share a generosity of spirit—an outlook that says, *I want to make the world a better place, and I'll do what I can to make that happen.*

My whole life, whenever problems came up, I always swept them under the rug. I'd always felt my job was to be positive. But I was hiding behind my smile. Being positive is one of my strengths, and it can be inspiring for others, but it can also be a mask for reality, which isn't always so pretty.

There are times, for example, when my body is in a lot of pain. People may not suspect that, since I generally smile through it. If I talk about it at all, I do my best to downplay it. It's important to me to keep going; after all, I'm used to physical discomfort, and I've got a job to do. But sometimes, when my bones and my joints just hurt, it can start feeling as if it's almost too much.

Still, even when I'm dealing with a lot of pain, I'll go along that way for quite a while, telling myself it's just because of my crazy schedule or that I'm doing too much and I need to take a little more rest. (Rest? What's that? It sounds nice!) When I'm traveling for work, I usually have to walk a lot, and that can make me achy. But I always try to suck it up and keep going.

In one way or another, I've always pushed myself beyond my limits, and I've come to realize this is very closely connected to my urge to please everyone. I want people around me to see that I'm okay and I don't need them to worry about me. I want everyone to know I'm fine, and I can handle it—whatever "it" might be.

This was my approach to cheerleading in high school. Talk about constant aches and pains throughout my entire body! That was when I first started hurting my foot, which has been an ongoing issue ever since. But I didn't stop. I couldn't! I just wanted to get out there, keep going, and keep up with my team. Even when my foot was really in bad shape and I had to wear a cast, I would walk on it when I wasn't supposed to.

Looking back, I roll my eyes and think, *What a teenager!* I was supposed to take my recovery periods very seriously and not cheat my way through them, but instead, I would tell myself my doctor didn't know what he was talking about. He was only a medical professional with many years of experience, right? I was the one who was living inside my body, and I knew my own limits. So I would go ahead and do exactly what he'd told me not to do.

That's when it all started, with my foot, at least. But keeping my chin up no matter what and pushing myself to show everyone I was okay, even when I wasn't, that began much earlier. My desire to please everyone and stay positive only progressed the older I got and the more I started taking on both professionally and medically. The more surgeries I had to have and the more professional obligations I took, the more stubborn I became about doing it all and smiling my way through it.

The urge to please others is something we all experience. Maybe it comes from childhood, when our parents are our whole world and all we want to do is make them happy. Childhood is about learning to follow the rules, but it's also about figuring out your personal strengths, often so you can gain attention and approval by doing what you do best. Sometimes, of course, it's not necessarily what you do best that gets you the attention you crave! When I was young, for example,

I always made my bed. I was too small to stretch the blanket all the way across, so I'm sure the result was far from perfect but I knew it made my mom happy, so I made a point of doing it every morning before school.

Our parents' disappointment can really sting, and their approval can feel like the best thing in the world. It's no wonder a lot of kids want to do whatever it takes to earn that gold star. And it's no wonder many people carry that urge to please and perform into adulthood.

In many ways, the urge to please is closely connected to the determination to overcome obstacles and succeed. Unfortunately, it's all too easy for that desire to turn into a mask that hides our true feelings. But pushing through adversity has a definite upside as well as a downside. There's certainly a lot about it that is wonderful and important. I couldn't accomplish even half of what I do if I didn't strive to maintain a positive outlook. And I know I learned that positive outlook from my dad. He's the most optimistic person I know, and he taught me to have that same attitude: to meet each day with enthusiasm for whatever lies ahead.

He really is a teacher in every aspect of his life. He motivates me and the rest of our family to keep our chins up. He inspires us to welcome every experience that life brings our way as a blessing, or at least a learning experience. He's done the same for countless students over his nearly thirty years as an educator.

It's funny—my dad has always loved school. Always! My aunts have told me about how he would force them to play School with him when they were kids. He would make them sit in chairs, and he would stand in front of them and teach them random things. He would even make my grandma have parent–teacher conferences so he could give her progress reports on my aunts! And he would get so mad if they didn't play along.

Teaching is definitely in his blood, as is that wonderful, positive attitude of his. Growing up, his role in his family was to keep everyone laughing, and that's a big part of his role in our family to this day. It definitely comes in handy, considering everything we've been through with my health, being bullied, and other struggles I've encountered in life.

Last year, my dad went with me to the doctor's appointment where we ended up scheduling surgery for my foot. It wasn't my first foot surgery, so I knew what to expect—which meant I knew it was going to be rough. For me, one of the worst parts of having surgery is the anticipation leading up to it. Every time I have a procedure scheduled, I know there's going to be a lot of pain, and I know the recovery is going to take time— time I could be using for work or other activities I'd much rather be doing than being laid up, sore, and miserable!

The surgeries I've had have been necessary, though. They're just part of my life and my regular health maintenance. Still, knowing that doesn't really help in the moment, when the prospect of yet another painful procedure looms over me.

The day of that doctor's appointment, I knew in my gut that we would probably have to schedule the foot surgery, and I really didn't want to do it. I was being kind of quiet in the car and in the waiting room before they called us in to see the doctor. I was so anxious! But thank goodness for my dad, who wouldn't let me stew in my anxiety. Instead, just like always, he made me laugh the entire time we were waiting and all through the appointment.

By the time the doctor confirmed that we couldn't let things with my foot go any longer and it was time to schedule the surgery, it wasn't even a big deal. I was calm, relaxed, and in a great mood because we'd been laughing the entire time.

My health issues have forced my family to learn how to keep things in perspective. We all rely on my dad's ability to keep us in good spirits. I want to be clear: Being able to make people laugh might seem like a simple, lighthearted, even superficial kind of thing, but it's a valuable skill. In fact, it is a gift that shows great depth and wisdom. Considering what my family and I have had to deal with my whole life, humor has come in handy again and again!

And my dad isn't faking it, either. When he's got that smile on his face and that twinkle in his eye, you know it's genuine. I'm so grateful for that special talent of his for brightening our world with laughter.

My dad isn't just Mr. Funny Guy, of course. He's also very kind and thoughtful. One Christmas, he got presents for all four of his sisters—nothing big, just baskets that he put little gifts into. He'd also tucked hand-written notes into each one, and as we drove to my grandma's house where the whole family was to gather, he read the cards out loud to us. They were so funny, but also so sweet! Later, I watched as he gave the cards to each of my aunts and they opened them. Each one of them cried. It was such a simple little thing that he'd done, but it made them so happy.

My aunts and my grandma started telling stories about my

dad when he was younger, about how thoughtful he'd always been. He was always trying to do things to help other people. Then he would go home and drive everyone crazy! He would pick on everyone and make them all mad, and that's exactly how he still is.

That same year, a few days after Christmas, my whole family was exhausted from the holidays—so of course my mom chose that moment to decide it was time to clean out the garage. She was probably right, but the timing wasn't perfect, because it was such a huge job. Their garage was so full of junk you couldn't even walk through it. To be fair, a lot of the mess was old clothes of Marina's and mine, as well as old papers and notebooks from school that were ripped and useless.

I knew a cleanup job that big meant my parents would be driving each other crazy, and they knew I wouldn't be much help, so we all agreed I would stay at my apartment and cheer them on from afar. For my part, I sent them pizza for dinner. (I mean, who doesn't love a good pizza?)

The next day, I texted my mom to see how things had gone. When she texted back how tired they were after cleaning, I responded, "After all that, I don't know how you two didn't kill each other!" The thing is, they're such a great team, but they're very different—everything from their basic personalities down to their cleaning styles. My dad's approach to cleaning is very sweeping: "Toss it all! Throw everything out!" My mom, on the other hand, always wants to save things or find someone to give them to.

My sister was there for the big cleanup job that day, so she saw it all, including the moment when they started snipping at each other. It went back and forth, just like always. Pretty soon, my mom was so mad, she refused to speak to my dad. Marina had to be the go-between, relaying messages back and forth between them, even though they were all in the same room. If my mom wanted something, Marina had to tell my dad, and if my dad wanted something, she had to tell my mom. It was all in fun, of course—well, mostly! In the entire time I've been on this earth, I've never seen those two stay mad at each other for longer than a day.

But like any married couple, they have their moments, and that day was one of them. At one point, my mom wanted her water, which happened to be near my dad. Marina asked him to pass her the water glass so she could give it to my mom.

Instead of giving her the water, my dad handed her a can of Raid. That accomplished exactly what my dad must have intended: It broke the tension in a split second. All three of them started laughing, and a minute later, my parents were talking to each other again, as if nothing had happened.

Later, we were laughing about it with a family friend. Our friend said, "Lupe is the only person I know who could be in such a tense situation and still find a way to make everyone laugh." She was right. That's just the kind of person he is.

———————

Our lives aren't all fun and games, even if they might appear that way from the outside. Even when I try to convince myself that's how it is, it's not. Something a lot of people may not suspect about me is that I've struggled with anxiety for years.

It may have been a part of me my whole life, but it

intensified several years ago, when a rough flight to Virginia really kicked it into gear. My dad was with me, and we were on one of those tiny puddle jumpers. What was supposed to be a simple thirty-minute flight turned into two hours of being stuck in the air in the midst of a storm, followed by an emergency landing that was bumpy, to say the least. People were screaming; the man sitting behind me threw up—I'll never forget that smell. Ever since then, I've had major anxiety on planes, and that's a pretty big problem for someone whose work involves frequent travel. I often take six or eight flights per month to meet my speaking commitments.

So when it came to dealing with my new airplane anxiety, I took the same approach I always took when problems came up: I simply ignored it as best I could. Along with plenty of other unpleasant things, I swept it under the rug.

After some personal reflection, I've realized that ignoring reality and staying positive—even when all I want to do is cry or scream—is a coping mechanism I've developed over time, but it's not always one that serves me.

We all need to give ourselves permission to feel our true feelings, even if those are decidedly darker or heavier than happiness. Instead of keeping that bright, positive attitude and claiming "I'm fine!" no matter what's really going on, we need to be honest, with ourselves and others, about how we're really feeling.

That's a lot more easily said than done. American culture is about one-upping each other, even in negative ways ("You had a bad day? Listen to what happened to *me*"). Many of us can see this play out every day in our Facebook feeds or on Instagram—the cultural phenomenon of people showing only their Best Of reels, life's most shining, picture-perfect moments, while excluding the more common, humdrum, often not-so-great moments that punctuate our everyday existence.

This seems almost like a cultural value we share as Americans. We love celebrities, and that Best Of reel happens naturally to them, whether they like it or not, purely because of the media. Their red-carpet moments are splashed across the tabloids, and people think that's their real lives.

I remember seeing an interview on Apple Music with the singer Adele. The interviewer asked about how her life has changed now that she's a world-famous superstar, and she said the main difference was what it's like to catch up with old friends. Now when she goes home and meets up with the friends she grew up with, she genuinely wants to know how they're doing and what they've been up to—but the first thing they always say is, "I'm doing fine, but it's nothing compared to all the wonderful things you're doing!" Those friends see the big, shining moments of her life playing out on TV and in the news, and they believe those represent her whole life—and their reality pales in comparison.

That bright, shiny picture, or face we present to the world? It's not real life. The trouble is, people can feel a real sense of depression and failure when their friends' lives appear so picture-perfect compared to their own, which fall far short of that ideal. The truth is, *no one's* life is perfect. It's all an act, one many of us buy into wholeheartedly.

Is this Best Of reel phenomenon particular to Americans?

I'm not sure. I only know that just about everyone I know seems invested in putting on a pretty face for friends and strangers alike, instead of being honest, genuine, and vulnerable about their true experiences.

When it comes to the Best Of reel, I used to be one of the worst offenders. It was tied to my people-pleasing personality, my urge to always put on a bright face and show others I was fine, no matter what was really going on.

Starting when I was just a little kid, I always wanted to make my parents believe I was fine, and nothing was wrong. They'd had enough to worry about since the moment I was born; I didn't want to add to it by complaining about anything, big or small.

Over time, I even began looking at it as my main job in life. Motivational speaking might be my career, but it was my *job* to stay positive! Positivity has always come easily to me, and it dovetails perfectly with my career. I feel obliged to present my audiences and fans with my personal example of emotional resilience, to show them they can stay strong in the face of their own struggles.

But I am very aware that I can't help anyone unless I help myself first. For me, it feels so much easier to help other people than it is to help myself. I would so much rather focus on that! That's why I developed my just-ignore-it strategy for dealing with anxiety. If I could pretend I wasn't having those feelings, then I could push forward with my work and my mission.

When it comes to conflict or problems or anything else that's scary to me, I'm the same way: I brush it under the rug so I don't have to deal with it until it explodes—or, preferably, until it disappears on its own. I definitely don't think this is the best strategy for dealing with fear, stress, or anxiety, and it's not something my parents taught or imposed on me. This is just the way I learned to handle things over time.

Whenever I've approached my parents with a problem that I needed to talk through, they've been amazing about helping me with it—but that hasn't happened very many times, because I don't like to let them in on my problems. My own weakness and vulnerability embarrass me. For some reason, over the years, I've saddled myself with this crazy expectation to be strong for everyone. That's why I can't acknowledge it when I have anxiety or doubts about myself: If I do, then I'm failing at my job. And I can't let that happen. I have too many people looking up to me to let them down.

Not everyone works as a motivational speaker, as I do; not everyone is in the public eye in the same way that I am, or has to so carefully consider the face they present to the world. Still, I don't think I am alone in this instinct to sweep problems under the rug and put on a bright face, even, or especially, during difficult times. It doesn't matter who you are or what you do for a living: I can almost guarantee that you receive messages constantly, from all sorts of sources, about the power of positive thinking and the importance of staying positive no matter what adversity you might face.

Staying strong is definitely an important value to learn. Finding success requires the ability to overcome challenges and adversity. At the same time, there's also reality: real life, real experiences, real emotions. Sometimes you just feel down, no matter how much you might try to pep yourself up.

One thing I've really struggled with is how to be strong and inspirational for others while still acknowledging that life can be really hard sometimes. I am constantly trying to balance the two, because it is so important to me to be honest and realistic about the way life truly is. I'm living it, just like you are. I'm sure you've been through some really hard times. I know I have, and I know I will again, because that's what life is all about: peaks and valleys, highs and lows.

When we received my diagnosis of neonatal progeroid syndrome, looking back, it seems strange to me that I stayed so calm during the meeting with my doctors. As we listened to my genetic doctor, Dr. Atul Chopra, explain the ins and outs of my condition, I remember being filled with the sense that having this extremely rare condition was my destiny. My parents didn't do anything that caused it. It wasn't something genetic they had passed along to me. As incredibly rare and unlikely as it was, it had simply happened spontaneously. And it had allowed me to help others who were born different.

I remember sitting at a large table in a conference room as Dr. Chopra explained all this complicated medical stuff about sequencing my twenty thousand genes and looking for mutations. He told us I had a "bad copy" of the *FBN1* gene, which affects my eyesight. Instantly, I thought, *It's not a bad copy—it's just my copy.* I still feel that way: My body and my genetic makeup are neither bad nor good. They're simply, uniquely mine.

I was following along with everything Dr. Chopra was

saying, yet I couldn't help feeling like I was waiting for the other shoe to drop. Where was the bad news? I knew it was coming. It had to be. But so far, my doctor was talking mostly about things I already knew. He and my other genetic doctor, Dr. Garg, had both suspected I had lipodystrophy, though at that point, it hadn't yet been confirmed. So when Dr. Chopra confirmed that was part of my diagnosis, it didn't come as a surprise.

But then he mentioned Marfan syndrome and neonatal progeroid syndrome and started listing off possible complications, including problems with my heart, bones, and vision.

There it was: The other shoe had dropped.

As he went on telling us about problems with my aortic valve that could result from my condition, I was filled with unease. What might happen to me? What else might he say? How bad was this diagnosis going to get?

Since I am a big believer in fate, it all started to make perfect sense. In that moment, it seemed clear that a very unique and unusual kind of gift had been given to me, and I was meant to use it for something important.

The thing that's so interesting about that to me now is this: My first impression was the truest, clearest thought I could possibly have had about my diagnosis. But almost instantly, fear and confusion crowded in, drowning out that inner sense of peace and certainty.

I confided in Sara a lot about my concern with no longer being the Undiagnosed Girl during the filming of our documentary. I'd had so many worries leading up to that doctor's visit. I'd done so much crying with Sara but always off camera. I definitely wasn't ready to open up about it in front of anyone except close friends.

Sara encouraged me to stay positive and promised no one would think less of my story because of the new diagnosis.

But even though wise, caring people in my life were telling me something I knew, deep down, was correct, I couldn't feel the truth of it in my heart.

Leading up to that meeting with Dr. Chopra, my anxiety just kept ratcheting up, higher and higher. I had so many crying sessions, both alone and with my closest friends, because I was so fearful that soon, no one would care anymore what I had to say. For the first time, I couldn't put on the mask of positivity. I had to admit it—I was scared.

CHAPTER 7

Breakdown or Break*through*?

Shame. It is a horrible, crippling emotion that rarely helps anyone, yet we all feel it at some point or another.

In this chapter, I'm going to reveal some deeply personal and potentially embarrassing stories, some of which are things I've never admitted or discussed with anyone before. Now I'm going to lay them all out in the pages of this book and do my best to manage any feelings of shame that may come from knowing the world now knows some of the most private moments of my life.

It's worth it to me to open a dialogue around these issues. The willingness to be honest and vulnerable can lead to a deeper understanding of each other and ourselves. It can help us become more compassionate toward those around us, as well as toward ourselves. I so admire anyone brave enough to be open about the moments in their lives they might rather have kept hidden, because their candor helps everyone feel more "normal" and less alone.

Shay Carl is a YouTube personality whose family is known as the first vlogging family of YouTube. Shay has been vlogging for years, and he's well known and respected. He's Mormon and very open about his faith. Last year, he released a podcast in which he admitted to being an alcoholic. I messaged him to tell him how much I respected his bravery in admitting that to his fans. In the podcast, he kept saying how important it is to live your truest story. That message resonated with me so deeply that I had a new bracelet made, stamped with the phrase *Live your story*.

Shay messaged me back: "Thank you so much for saying that and sharing that, Lizzie! I think sharing our vulnerabilities is really the answer to strengthening everyone! Love you!!!"

I loved that so much! That message of his—*live your truest story*—became an important reminder and encouragement to me as I worked on this book. I wore my *Live your story* bracelet to give me strength, knowing that soon, people around the world would be reading mine.

With that said, here we go . . .

———

Times of crisis—when everything in your life seems to be exploding and going crazy, and you feel as if you're gasping for air, barely able to keep your head above water—happen to everyone, unfortunately. It's almost unavoidable that you'll experience a breakdown of some kind, at some point. But breakdowns don't have to be a bad thing! I truly believe that, now that I've learned to look at my own breakdown as a personal break*through*.

It took a long time to view it in that light. I certainly couldn't see a silver lining in the moment, when my lifelong habit of brushing aside unpleasant feelings ended up leading to the biggest, scariest breakdown I've ever experienced.

It truly was one of the toughest periods of my life, and I'm still struggling to understand what happened. There wasn't just one trigger that I can point to that led up to it; a variety of factors came together to create the perfect storm for me to completely unravel.

First of all, it was hard on everyone, especially me, when we stopped shooting the documentary. For nine months, I had lived and breathed our filming schedule. I'd spent nearly every waking moment with Sara, Jessica Chou, who was the film's line producer, and the rest of the crew. We all hung out constantly, and together we lived and breathed everything involved in making the movie happen.

That meant we spent lots of time together at airports, exploring new hotels, or just spending hours together in front of our laptops. I loved all the times when Jessica, Sara, and I would get ready together for events, doing our hair and makeup and deciding on which shoes and dresses to wear. I even loved the times when we'd just hang out in a hotel room and order room service. I felt blessed to become so close with two such incredibly smart, strong, savvy women as we worked together on a project that was near and dear to all of our hearts.

Looking back now, I can see that during those intense months, I was enveloped in a kind of cocoon—a warm, protective shelter of kindness and connection. Before that, I'd always gotten that love and protection from my family, but the filming of our documentary was really the first time I got to experience it on my own terms, as a full-fledged adult. With Jessica and Sara by my side, I could go out on the town and enjoy myself like any twentysomething would, while benefitting from the wonderful buffer zone they provided between me and the world.

Leaving filming meant going back out into the cold, where I distinctly did not want to be. I wanted to be back in that cocoon again, back in that caring, close community I so loved being a part of.

Even more than that, I had gotten used to the rhythm of working nonstop. During that nearly yearlong period, I had coordinated my busy speaking schedule with my even busier filming schedule, and I'd reached brand-new levels in my career. I'd traveled to Capitol Hill to meet with members of Congress and lobby for an antibullying bill. I'd spoken to the largest audience of my entire speaking career so far. These were the biggest things I'd ever accomplished, and they were beyond my wildest dreams.

And then, suddenly, there was an abrupt stop to all of it when the film shoot was over. Sara and Jess and the rest of the crew had gotten all the raw footage they needed. Now it was time for them to move on to the next stages of polishing the film and getting it out in front of audiences. My part of the project was done, and I had no idea—none—what to do with myself or my free time.

I went back home to Austin to my little apartment. The first few days were okay, but then things got really *not* okay, fast.

The truth is, before that period, I had never been alone in my apartment for more than a day or two at a time. With the constant travel required by my job, I never had time to sit for hours on end, staring at the wall and feeling all my emotions and anxieties crowding in on me. But that was exactly what happened when I went home and, for the first time in memory, had more than a few long, empty days to myself.

At first, sleeping in, watching TV, and catching up on doing nothing felt fantastic. But the euphoria lasted a few days, at most. Once the shine wore off of being lazy, I was ready to get back to work. The only problem was, there was no work for me to do.

I tried reaching out to my family and my old friends, but everyone was busy. My parents and siblings had school or their jobs to go to every day. Connecting with my friends wasn't as easy as I'd hoped, maybe because I'd been gone for so long. We'd lost touch, and they were now also busy with work, children, and their daily routines.

I felt so alone. Since I don't drive, I was stuck at my apartment. My sense of isolation became so intense and overwhelming, it was almost suffocating. I started overthinking everything, asking myself these huge, awful, unanswerable questions: *Why do I feel so lonely? All my dreams are coming true, so why am I not happy? How can I help and inspire other people if I can't even help myself?*

Social media wasn't helping me feel any less lonely. In fact, it was making things worse. For some reason, I'd started letting people's negative comments on Twitter and my YouTube videos get to me. Ninety-eight percent of the time, I don't let those comments bother me, but there are still times when the nastier ones just hit me—almost as if by physical force, right through the screen. It's worse when I'm feeling sad; in those moments, it can really knock me down.

That was what was happening. I was all by myself, feeling low, and going online became another way to torture myself and dwell in the darkness of my own mind. I would latch on to some nasty comment and replay it over and over in my head. I'd get stuck on it—and suddenly, I was using it as a way to validate how sad I was feeling.

Most of all, my medical diagnosis was weighing heavily on my mind. This was really the first time I'd had spare time to start processing it emotionally. Until this point, I'd stayed so busy that I hadn't had the time or mental space to think about it much.

Of course, I had stayed that busy on purpose, because I hadn't wanted to confront the diagnosis or acknowledge what it meant. Like always, it had seemed easier if I just swept it under the rug. For months after receiving the diagnosis, I hadn't wanted to Google it, or look anything up, or read any articles about it. Most of all, I hadn't wanted to confront the fear that, somehow, the diagnosis would make me different.

But sweeping things under the rug only works for so long. All of a sudden, my diagnosis was on my mind constantly. I couldn't stop agonizing about what it meant for my health, my future, my family, my career—and for my identity, the very core of who I thought I was. Would people still think I was special when they found out my condition wasn't quite as rare as we had all thought?

The issue that gradually became the biggest and most profound piece of the puzzle was this: I now had to face the heavy realization of what it truly meant to have a serious health condition, one that could become an emergency situation at any moment. For twenty-five years, my parents and I hadn't even known I had a heart condition at all. Now, all of a sudden, we knew I had one, we knew it was serious, and we knew it was part of an entire *syndrome*. It was mind-boggling. I could hardly wrap my head around it.

But one element kept bothering me, actually keeping me up at night: The fact that the heart condition was the wild card. For all these years, we hadn't known what we were dealing with when it came to my health. Now life seemed scarier and less certain than ever.

With my particular heart condition, the risk is that my aortic valve might dilate to the point of abruptly rupturing. Beyond scheduling regular checkups with my cardiologist, there is no way to know if or when my heart condition might become critical. That was what was so frightening about it to me. The entire situation was completely out of my control. I had never before had to face the prospect of my own mortality so head-on.

All my life, I had worried about being a burden to my family. That was why I'd worked so hard to be as strong and independent as possible. It seemed cruelly ironic that now, when I'd finally taken significant strides toward greater independence, I was suddenly more worried than ever about burdening the people I loved. If the worst happened and I was suddenly gone, it would be their greatest fear come true. How would my parents and the rest of my family handle that?

With all of these thoughts, worries, and dark emotions, my anxiety spiraled out of control.

Here's one of the details about my personal life that I'm embarrassed to admit: Sometime before all this, I had developed a habit of pulling my hair. I've never revealed that before in any public forum. Though there have been so many times when I've wanted to talk about it in a blog post or a video, I've never had the courage to do it because it felt too humiliating to admit I was harming myself in such a tangible way. I couldn't stand the shame.

As my anxiety worsened, my hair pulling started getting really bad. You could actually see the spots where I had been pulling it out. I was deeply embarrassed to discuss this with my doctor, but when I did, he was so wonderful about it. He explained it was just a nervous habit, and he assured me that a lot of people do it. He gave me a special shampoo and a topical cream to help repair my damaged scalp, and wrote me a prescription for antianxiety medication to take whenever I needed it, especially when I was going to fly. I was confident the things he prescribed would help me overcome those barriers, but I had no idea they would lead me down a completely unexpected road.

The medication I was taking was so strong that it would just knock me out. I would sleep for hours on end, which could be kind of wonderful because I was feeling so terrible— exhausted, lost, lonely, and sad—but if I took a pill, I didn't have to feel that way. It was like magic: I could just take a pill and not have to think about anything at all. I wouldn't feel stressed about anything. I could just sleep.

I started taking more and more pills every day. Over time, without even really realizing what was happening or how I had let it occur, I found myself hooked on my anxiety medication.

I told myself I was just using the pills to sleep, but the reality was that I was using them to sleep *all the time*. I was sleeping all day, every day, in order to avoid my true, messy, difficult feelings—feelings of fear and vulnerability, of loneliness and depression, and of deep, raw despair.

Looking back, I now realize I was trying to speed up, however unconsciously, what I saw as the inevitable. If I was just going to devastate my family someday by dying from this heart condition, I would rather it happen sooner than later. I didn't want to be a burden on them; I didn't want them to have to worry indefinitely about the terrible outcome that would eventually come.

For the first time in my life—and I hope the only time—I had suicidal thoughts. It seems so crazy now, but at the time, I truly thought that if I just went to sleep in my big, soft, comfy bed and simply didn't wake up, that would spare everyone I loved from having to deal with the inevitable later on.

Never before had I had such dark thoughts and emotions. I was irritated all the time; I'd lost a lot of weight, which is especially concerning for someone with lipodystrophy; and there are many days from that period that I have no memory of whatsoever. I became someone else. No one who knew me could recognize this new person as the Lizzie I'd always been.

My younger sister, Marina, was attending college at Texas State, where I had gone to school just a few years earlier. When she came home one weekend, several weeks into my dark cloud, she could tell something was really wrong. There were bruises all over my legs because I kept falling and running into things—which, of course, I didn't remember doing. One day I had put a pot on the stove and turned it on; I must have decided to make something, although I have no idea what because I don't remember doing it. My sister came into my apartment and discovered the pot sitting on the burner, its plastic handle melting. Thinking about that still makes me shudder. The whole apartment complex could have burned down. It could have been a huge disaster. Not only was I putting myself in danger, but I was unknowingly putting those around me in harm's way as well.

It's easier to recognize now how desperate and desolate I was feeling. All my dreams were coming true, yet at the same time I was forced to look into this mirror of mortality and face the fact that it could all be gone in a moment—that I, too, could be gone in a moment. Everything in my life was so incredible, but my diagnosis made all of it—my accomplishments, everything I was working so hard to achieve—seem like it didn't matter one bit.

At the time, I believed that was it. If all that wonderfulness wasn't enough to make me happy, then there was no hope that anything could ever make me happy, ever again. I stopped caring. I reached the lowest point I had ever reached in my entire life, and I was ready to throw in the towel.

All the conditions leading to my breakdown had come together to create the perfect storm: the complicated, difficult ending of my relationship with Blake; my growing loneliness and unhappiness; my ongoing issues with anxiety and growing dependence on my anxiety medication; the end of the shooting schedule for the documentary; the dark, negative thoughts that grew within me in the months after I received my diagnosis; and the pressure I was still putting on myself to stay positive through it all, so that my parents, close friends, and fans wouldn't worry about me.

Everything finally came to a head when my sister found my pill bottles in my nightstand.

I have no idea how she knew to look there or even when she looked. I have no idea what tipped her off. All I know is we spent the day together at my apartment, and she could tell I was acting weird. She could tell I was just *off*, and somehow, she knew to trust her instincts to figure out what was going on.

I am so grateful to her for that. We all need someone who knows and loves us like that—someone who knows exactly what we're really thinking and feeling, just by the expression on our faces. Marina is one of those people in my life, and I am so thankful for her.

When she found my pills in my nightstand, she called our parents and told them what she'd found, and then she brought me to their house. As soon as we got there, I fell asleep in their bed. When I woke up, Sara was there; Marina had called her to tell her what was going on.

Later, Sara told me that she and I had talked on the phone that evening, though I have no recollection whatsoever of that conversation. She said I'd been speaking in words she couldn't understand—that my intonation had sounded almost normal, but it was as if the words I was saying weren't in any language that actually existed.

Marina saved my life that day. Even though she is my younger sister, she instinctively took care of me in a very serious situation, and her efforts were a wonderful example of kindness. Growing up, we were just like typical sisters. We would drive each other crazy! Marina would always come into my room when I was hanging out with my friends, and I would have to beg my mom to make her leave. My parents always told us that when we grew up, we were going to be best friends— and I'm happy to say, they were right. There will never be enough words for me to thank Marina for what she did that day. I can't imagine the fear she must have felt, seeing me like that. We both have a lot of our mom's caretaking instincts, and on that particular day, Marina's shone as brightly as a light.

Later that night, after I woke up in my parents' bed, my mom told me to go lie on the couch in the living room. When I got there, I found Sara already sitting on the couch, and my parents sitting side by side. I could tell we were about to have a serious discussion.

I still don't remember the entire conversation. I know lots of things came up about how hard the transition had been on everybody, not just me, when we finished shooting the documentary. The main thing I remember is crying, and crying, and then crying some more.

After we had that big sit-down talk at my parents' house, I knew my first step was to stop taking the pills. And I did it—cold turkey. Once again, Marina became a huge light for me during that time. I was still very ashamed to talk to my parents about what I had been doing, but Marina made it so easy for me to depend on her. By this time she was back at her college campus, yet she still made it a point to check on me multiple times a day.

As I slowly returned to my old self, we both started relying on each other. We would share our daily schedules, goals, and challenges, and we'd cheer each other on whenever we woke up happy and ready to take on the day. Who knew such a terrifying experience would bring my little sister and me closer than ever before? She became one of my heroes during one of the darkest periods of my life.

I want to note here that the way I stopped taking my meds—doing it cold turkey—isn't necessarily the way everyone should do it. When you're on medication to treat anxiety or depression and you want to stop taking the meds, make sure you do it according to your doctor's instructions and the specific requirements of the type of medication you've been taking. Certain medications are very dangerous to stop cold turkey and require a weaning-off process.

That being said, the type of medication I'd been taking was safe to stop abruptly, and quitting that way actually wasn't that tough—at least, not physically. I had a few days of feeling like crap, but there was no real harm done by stopping the meds altogether.

Far more difficult than the physical withdrawal symptoms was confronting and dealing with my feelings again, for the first time in months—maybe even years. Suddenly, my emotions were completely out of whack, and it was a very harsh reality. I hadn't realized I'd been completely numb until, suddenly, I was feeling it all again. It was overwhelming, and I didn't know how to handle it.

Many people have experienced what I was going through. A lot of us turn to using different types of Band-Aids to cover up overwhelming feelings when life gets really tough. Trying to escape those feelings can seem normal or natural; it's the way I've always done it. But it obviously isn't the best way. There are so many resources out there to turn to for help, to find your way back to physical and mental health, so you can be okay again.

Whether you're struggling with suicidal thoughts, substance abuse, overwhelming emotions like sadness, depression, anger, or anything else, you can find support. Whether it's your doctor, a therapist, a good friend, a support group, or even a hotline, it's so important to reach out and ask for help.

Most of all, don't be ashamed. Let go of your shame, so you can reach out and get the help you need. That is the most critical piece of the puzzle to me. No matter what you did or what you're going through, I guarantee you aren't the only one. Instead of focusing on your embarrassment, focus on feeling eager and excited to make positive changes in your life. Focus on how proud you'll feel when you come out on the other side!

That's easy to say, but pretty tough to do. At first, I didn't know what to do. I would just sit in my apartment in the dark and never open the blinds on my windows. It took some time, but I finally did start opening my blinds. To let the light in, both literally and figuratively, and acknowledge the day was a critical step. I hadn't been doing that, but once I started, other, tentative forward steps followed.

I slowly started getting back on my YouTube channel. That was overwhelming at first, because there were a ton of comments from my followers and fans: "We've missed you! Where have you been?" That felt great, but it also fed into my hang-up about responsibility. I thought I had neglected a huge group of people that I really cared about, and that felt awful. It is both humbling and surreal for me to realize that for many of my viewers and fans, my YouTube channel is one of the only places where they can connect, share their personal stories, and be incredibly real and honest about their feelings and experiences. When I dropped out, I left them out in the cold, and I will always regret that.

This difficult experience actually led to a positive change in me, however, and in the videos I started posting. I had always been afraid to be honest and vulnerable in my videos about the tough times, so I would censor my feelings. Looking back, I think I was actually trying to control the comments people posted. If I didn't self-censor my videos—if I was really *real*, truly open about what I was feeling, even when it wasn't pretty—I was scared of how people might react.

But after my breakdown, I finally started opening up anyway and just being real. When I was feeling overwhelmed and sad, I didn't hide it anymore. Instead, I would turn on the camera and start filming. There are now plenty of videos of me crying and talking about what I'm going through. Believe me, it makes me really uncomfortable to put those out there for everyone to see—yet I'm so proud of those videos, too.

I'm also very thankful we don't have smell-vision yet, because some mornings, I don't even bother to brush my teeth before I start filming a new video! I just roll out of bed, put in my contact lens, grab my camera from my nightstand, and start talking to the little black box with its recording light blinking.

Go figure—those are the videos that my YouTube followers connect with the most.

Initially, after my breakdown, I was hit with a huge wave of guilt. I felt like I'd let myself down, I'd let my family down, I'd let my friends down…But once I let go of my guilt, I started feeling profoundly grateful.

There have always been tons of things I can relate to and help people with: feelings of sadness and loneliness, of guilt and shame, of anger. But there had always been one thing I could understand but not really relate to on a personal level, and that was the feeling of just wanting to give up. My own struggle with suicidal thoughts has helped me connect with other people who are stuck feeling the same way.

When I post those videos, the ones in which I'm really open about how I'm feeling, I've been so pleasantly surprised by how many people post comments about their personal struggles. I can't tell you how good it feels to go back a day later and see the support and the community represented in those comments. Technically, we're all strangers to each other on my YouTube channel, yet everyone is so real and supportive. It feels incredible that I started that, as scary as it was for me. Even though the people posting comments aren't in front of the camera, a lot of them are being incredibly vulnerable in sharing their stories, and I love that they're feeling safe enough to reveal that side of their reality.

Vulnerability is so important, and it's essential to have a community or person you can be vulnerable with. That's what keeps us sane! Just a few days after the big, difficult talk at my parents' house, Sara and I spent an evening with Alexis Jones, one of our documentary's executive producers, and her fiancé. Afterward, Sara drove me home, and I had another big, cleansing breakdown in her car, in the parking lot at my apartment complex.

I remember sitting there, clutching her hand, just crying and crying and crying. It felt as if I couldn't stop—as if the tears would never end. Sara wasn't afraid of my flood of emotions. She just held my hand and allowed me that safe space to let it all out.

I will forever be grateful for that. Angels come into your life at the perfect moment—and what a strange, random moment that was: Late at night, after having been out having fun with our close friends, and then there we were, sitting in Sara's car, holding hands as I let out all this desperation and misery. In that moment, I knew Sara had gone from being just regular Sara to being Sara, my guardian angel, who literally held my hand through a brief but intense storm of pain.

I'm really glad I had a trusted friend with me in my dark moment. I had never felt such deep, intense emotional pain before, that sense of wanting to give up because going on felt impossible. But now that I have felt it—and, by the grace of God, nothing truly bad or irrevocable happened as a result—I can use that experience to help other people. I can say to others who are going through the same thing, "This is what it felt like to me, this is how I got through it, and you are truly not alone."

In those tough moments, the bravest thing you can do is reach out, admit what's happening, and ask for help.

CHAPTER 8

How a Dog Named Ollie Saved My Life

This brings us to a small, playful, scruffy little dog named Ollie.

To understand the significance of this little guy in my life, it's important to understand that my family has always taken care of me, my entire life. I'm a grown woman, in my late twenties, but there are still many things my parents help me with on a regular basis. When they found out I'd been abusing my anxiety medication, it raised a giant red flag for them, and they became extremely afraid for my well-being.

I wasn't any more certain or secure about myself or my future than they were. During our big talk at my parents' house, my parents said they didn't want me living alone any longer, but I didn't want to find a roommate or live with anyone else. We were at an impasse—until, at some point during the discussion, someone suggested I get a dog.

I'd always wanted a dog, but since college, I'd thought I was too busy to take care of one. Still, the moment that the suggestion was made, I was on board. And then, in an example of that mysterious synchronicity that sometimes makes the right thing happen at just the right time, my mom texted me a couple of weeks later to tell me a woman from our church was looking for a home for a puppy.

My mom sent along a picture of the dog. As soon as I saw the photo, I fell in love with that little bundle of whitish-silver fur. She'd also texted me a link where I could find out more about the puppy online, and when I visited the site, I saw another photo of him. In this one, he was sitting on a couch surrounded by a bunch of toys, and there was something about him that grabbed me and wouldn't let go. Right away, he stole my heart! I watched a video of him jumping up to catch a treat. After he caught it, his tongue flew out of his mouth, making him look like he had a huge smile on his face.

Immediately, I texted my mom back, "I love him. I want him. I'm going to get him."

Within two days, my parents brought the puppy to my apartment so I could meet him. In person, I fell in love even more deeply than I had when I saw his picture. And that's how it happened: Suddenly, I was the proud owner of a little dog named Oliver.

It wasn't easy—at least, not at first. I was so nervous! I'd never had to care for a dog all on my own before, and suddenly, here was Ollie: little, adorable, hyper Ollie, who needed to be fed and walked and played with and cleaned up after almost constantly, it seemed. But I was determined to show everyone I could do it.

The next night, my good intentions were foiled when a sudden health emergency sent me to the hospital. That was such a blow. In a way, I was used to impromptu trips to the hospital, but this time, the timing couldn't have been worse. I'd been so set on showing my family that I could be responsible for this furry little being, and the second day, there I was, in the hospital, needing their help to care for him.

It was a bumpy beginning, to say the least. Once again, the people closest to me came through for me in a big way. Jessica stayed at my apartment while I was in the hospital, and she took good care of Ollie for me. She even sent me videos of him playing, which made me feel so much better! A couple days later, I was back home again and on the mend, and Ollie and I were overjoyed to see each other.

Taking care of Ollie definitely helped distract me from sinking into any heavy feelings I was dealing with. This was the first time I had ever been responsible for keeping someone else besides myself alive, and I'm not going to lie: At first, I was terrified. But like so many other challenges in life, it was truly a blessing. On the days when I just wanted to stay in bed and cry, this little dog kept me from feeling sorry for myself. He wouldn't let me retreat from the world; he forced me to get up and get moving.

Soon enough, taking care of Ollie became second nature. I loved it so much, even when I got sick or sank into a funk. No matter what happens or how I'm feeling, I still have to take care of Ollie. In fact, those are the times when I'm especially grateful for that scrappy little fur ball. Even when I'm sick and in bed, I have to get up and feed him and take him outside to run around. That's been the biggest help, because it forces me to stay active and engaged. Besides, it's not as if it's something I don't enjoy doing. Making Ollie feel better makes me feel better, too. We go hand in hand, and it really works.

Even more than that, Ollie has helped me overcome a lot of the fears I used to have. Initially, it scared me to take him to the dog park when other people were there with their dogs. If Ollie started barking or getting too excited, would I be strong enough to manage the situation on my own? That was my biggest fear as a new dog owner. The truth is, I'm still working on overcoming that one—Ollie's a little hyper!—but we're working on it.

Then there's the issue of strangers in the dog park. I used to feel so nervous to be around them. I never knew if I should talk to them or not. I always felt so shy. But I overcame that and started striking up brief conversations with people. That may seem like a small thing, but it's something that I'm really grateful to Ollie for. Because of him, I've had to put myself into situations that have taken me beyond my comfort level—situations that aren't just about taking care of my dog but that have allowed me to grow as a person.

I even decided to move to an apartment with a backyard so Ollie could have more time to play outside. That decision was a big one. Having my rent increase solely for Ollie to have a better quality of life was a decision I never expected I'd be in a position to make—but it's nothing I wouldn't do for any other family member, and Ollie has truly become a member of the family. I love that! My first Christmas with him, many of the gifts under my tree were marked "With Love from Lizzie and Ollie." That's how integral to he'd already become my life. We were a team from the very beginning.

Best of all, my parents and siblings love him just as much as I do. Since my schedule is busier these days than it's ever been before, they help take care of him when I have to travel for work. Sometimes they dog-sit just for fun, even when I'm not away on business. My sister, Marina, especially likes taking him for the weekend every now and then.

That's always a little weird for me—being completely alone in my apartment when Ollie goes for a play date with my family. It doesn't happen often, but when it does, it highlights the fact that, when you have a pet, you're never *truly* alone. You always have a beloved little friend there for company. When Ollie is gone for a day or two, it's so strange to not have him right behind me or sitting at my feet. It may sound funny, but he's become such an important part of my life that things are just not the same without him. When he's not there, it feels like I'm missing my shadow.

I truly believe everyone needs a pet, especially if you're dealing with loneliness, depression, or anxiety. We can learn a lot from animals—not just unconditional love, but also forgiveness, optimism, playfulness, and how to enjoy the simple things. Most of all, a dog or a cat can bring so much unconditional love and kindness to your life, and having someone to love just makes the world feel like a kinder, gentler place.

CHAPTER 9

The Knowing

Before Dr. Chopra gave us my diagnosis, I used to fantasize about what it would be like to know what, exactly, I had and why I was the way I was. I had no idea what that might feel like—The Knowing. That was how I had come to think of it: *The Knowing*, capital *T*, capital *K*. Through the years, the medical tests and specialists, and searching for answers, I never, ever thought I would actually get to know. Maybe that's why it rocked my world at such a fundamental level once I finally did.

I've come to believe that with all major life transitions comes a breakthrough into a new level of knowledge—a new level of Knowing. Think about your own life: What difficult, even traumatic experiences have you gone through? What have you struggled to learn, find out, or understand about yourself or about life? Whatever tough things you've experienced, I'm willing to bet you reached a new level of understanding as a result. It may have taken some time—even a long time—and a lot of struggle and self-reflection, but I'll bet there was a lesson waiting for you, when you were ready to receive it.

That's how it was for me after receiving my diagnosis. The diagnosis and the breakdown that followed cracked me open in some terrifying ways. Ultimately, though, those experiences transformed into a break*through*, one that taught me some truly important lessons about myself and life itself. And my breakthrough caused a significant shift in my conception of *The Knowing*.

The insight I gained from The Knowing turned out to be this: Just like everyone else, I have been rare and special all along. I didn't need a diagnosis or a percentage or a set of statistics to prove that. What I thought was so critical to my "brand"—being a rarity, being known as the Undiagnosed Girl—wasn't really a big deal at all. I thought people were paying attention to me because I was an enigma. I didn't understand that they were paying attention to me because I had something important to say, something they wanted to hear.

I learned something else important, too: When it comes to medical issues, you never really know what can happen, and you definitely don't have any control. There are always new advances in medicine and new discoveries related to human health. Just when I think I've finally got the answers I've been seeking, something new and unexpected crops up.

Dr. Chopra contacted me again in 2016, nearly two years after he delivered the news of my diagnosis to my family and me. This time, he e-mailed my parents and me to tell us he had some new test results he wanted to discuss with us.

That e-mail came as quite a surprise. The truth is, when I read it, I had no idea what he was talking about. I hadn't had any medical testing done in over two years, so I certainly wasn't expecting any new test results to surface.

My parents and I scheduled a time to talk with him, and then I promptly put the whole thing out of my mind. I didn't know what Dr. Chopra could possibly have to tell me, but I had a feeling it was going to be something big. Until I could speak with him directly about it, I didn't want to think about it. I didn't want to dwell on it or let anxiety about whatever it might be overwhelm me. Besides, Dr. Chopra hadn't asked us to drive to Houston to meet with him, as we'd done when he gave us my diagnosis. He'd just asked us to give him a call to discuss whatever it was. I figured that meant it couldn't be anything too terrible.

When the day of the phone conference finally arrived, my parents came to my apartment so we could make the call together. As soon as we got Dr. Chopra on the phone, the first thing he said to me was, "You have nothing to worry about. I figured that would be the best way to start this call. Everything is okay, so you don't need to worry."

I thought that was funny and sweet, and it was definitely a big relief.

Then he launched into why he had called, and I learned that I'd been exactly right: It wasn't anything bad, but it was definitely something very, very big.

Several years earlier, Dr. Chopra had performed lots of different medical tests on me leading up to my diagnosis of NPS. For one test, I had to go to "hospital jail"—a twenty-four-hour period when I had to stay by myself in a tiny room, with no human contact whatsoever, while Dr. Chopra measured all kinds of things: how much oxygen I was taking in, what I was eating and drinking, everything.

I'll never forget how much I hated being in hospital jail. I'll definitely never forget how much I hated the food! I hardly ate anything, because everything tasted disgusting. I remember feeling like the whole test was a waste of time, because I hadn't eaten normally and I hadn't been in my usual environment. What could they really tell from all those random measurements, anyway?

More than two years later, I spoke with Dr. Chopra on the phone, and that question was finally answered.

He informed me that he and some other doctors and researchers continued studying those test results from back when I'd been in hospital jail. That cracked me up—that he referred to it as hospital jail, just as I'd always done. Dr. Chopra has a way of meeting me on my own level, and he definitely has a sense of humor—two qualities I really appreciate about him.

He told me they found six other people in the United States who also have NPS. Those six people had all gone to hospital jail, too, to have the same measurements taken that I had done. All of our combined test results led Dr. Chopra and his team to some very big findings.

I can't relay word for word what he told us on the phone that day. He was communicating in doctor-speak, using lots of big words I didn't understand to describe what he and his team found. The basic gist of it, as I understood it, was this: First, he had discovered that all seven of us Americans with

NPS also have hypoglycemia. That was news to me, but it made sense. There are times when I feel like I have to inhale chocolate, so it wasn't a huge surprise to learn I have chronically low blood sugar.

Second, they found that all seven of us were missing a part of a certain hormone that helps people gain weight. Dr. Chopra told me they were still working on getting everything cleared, legally and medically, but once that happened, he said it was possible that I would be able to have injections that would address that hormonal deficiency, change my appetite, and ultimately help me gain weight.

That particular piece of news made me incredibly emotional. It came out of the blue, so unexpectedly—just like the original diagnosis of NPS two years earlier. Just as I had never, ever expected we would actually receive a diagnosis, I had also never, ever thought something like this could happen: that new medical advances might be made that would affect my condition or that might help us address some of my biggest health issues.

Am I explaining the gravity of that moment well enough? For over twenty-five years, I had been working on accepting the reality of my ongoing health issues and convincing myself that I wouldn't change one single thing about myself, even if I could. Many people had asked me over the years whether I would, if I could, take a magic pill that would make me gain weight. I had always said I wouldn't, because I don't want to change the way I look. I don't want to change one single thing about myself. As I've said so many times before, I truly feel that I was meant to have this incredibly rare condition, and having it has informed everything about who I am: my experiences, my worldview, my career...everything.

To suddenly be faced with the prospect of possibly being able to improve my health and even change my appearance...I didn't know what to think. It was seriously mind-blowing, and as confusing as anything I'd ever faced before.

There was another element adding to my confusion: The hormone injections Dr. Chopra was describing to me were brand-new and completely untested on humans. That meant, if I decided to move forward with them, there would be no way to know beforehand what the potential might be for either benefits or risks to my health.

Instantly, my mind was reeling. Did I want to be that guinea pig? Dr. Chopra had just told us there were six other people in the United States who had the same syndrome I had. Why couldn't they be the guinea pigs? Why did it have to be me?

Of course I knew that was a pretty uncharitable way of looking at the situation, but in the moment, it was hard to see it any other way. It was just so much to take in all at once. Dr. Chopra told me the findings of his research were due to be published the following week in a medical journal. He assured me he wouldn't share my personal information in any public way, but he added, "Our PR team knows about you, and they know you're a public figure. Would you like to be interviewed or give a quote that could be used in the journal article?"

If I hadn't been reeling, I might have laughed out loud. It

had taken me so many months to be able to admit aloud that my medical condition had finally been diagnosed—and now Dr. Chopra was asking me to give a quote for an article, or maybe even an interview? The idea of talking about it so publicly and so soon boggled my mind. I needed to wrap my brain around it before I could discuss it any further.

My parents were incredibly excited about the news, but I just felt like, *Slow down. Give me a second—I need to think about this.*

It had taken me so long to get comfortable with my diagnosis. Now, all of a sudden, I was supposed to switch tracks all over again so I could hurtle toward a wildly unexpected and uncertain future.

Dr. Chopra's call was really funny timing in more ways than one. When he called, I'd had surgery on my foot a couple weeks earlier and had already been on two business trips since then, even though I was still recuperating. Ollie had been staying with my parents instead of at home with me, since between traveling and recuperating, I couldn't care for him on my own. But not having him around was tough. I kept feeling like a crazy person—I mean, he's just a dog!—yet his absence really showed me how much I had come to rely on him since he'd first come to live with me.

It didn't take long for me to realize that the call with Dr. Chopra occurred on almost the exact anniversary of when I'd adopted Ollie. Now, nearly a year to the day later, my head was spinning all over again with so much new information, so many questions and so many weighty decisions to be made, that not having Ollie with me was almost too much. I really

needed him. Without him, I was alone at my apartment, trying to deal with these overwhelming feelings.

It was hard not to feel as if I'd just taken a giant step backward in time. It was as if all the hard work I'd done in the past
year, putting my life back together after my breakdown, was
suddenly unraveling. It was hard not to fear that I might be
heading right back to that dark, dark place all over again.

It also felt like déjà vu from when we'd originally found
out about my diagnosis, two years earlier. It was definitely yet
another reminder that there's just no warning when it comes
to my health. These things simply happen, and every time, I
have to find a way to roll with it. But sometimes that can be
really, really hard to do.

I understood that Dr. Chopra's findings promised to be
really good news for a lot of people. He kept congratulating
me during the phone call, telling me, "Now you're going to be
able to help so many people with medical issues like diabetes
and obesity." I was glad to hear that, of course, but at the
same time, I couldn't help thinking, *What about me?*

My mental response was selfish, but I couldn't help it. It
was that same lab rat feeling that I knew all too well. When
you have a major, rare medical diagnosis, you have to get all
these tests done, but sometimes you can't help but wonder
whether it's really helping you. I didn't ask to come into this
life with any of the circumstances I was born into—neither
the wonderful ones, like my family, nor the challenging ones,
like my diagnosis.

Because I was born into those circumstances, I am in a
position of bearing a big responsibility to help other people on

a lot of levels. And a large part of that I have fully embraced: Helping people on an emotional level is my life's work, my calling. My greatest hope is that I can help make the world a better place for everyone.

But there is definitely another part of my responsibility that I have not yet fully embraced, and that includes the physical, medical part—that lab rat feeling that I've had so many times in my life. Being in this position is tough, even though I believe I am here for a reason.

I've thought a lot about why this is such a big deal to me, and I've come to realize, once again, that it's all about control. When I was younger and I was being bullied, I was able to take control of that by turning it around and making something positive come of it. But with medical issues, you can't really take control of that. You can't create your own outcome. You just have to put one foot in front of the other and go by what your doctor says.

From the time I was born and throughout my childhood, my doctors didn't know of anyone else in the world who had the same condition I did. There was no one to compare me to. Everything they did to try to help me was basically a shot in the dark. All the tests they ran were gathering completely new data, in search of a diagnosis that no one truly thought would ever come.

Suddenly, with Dr. Chopra's call, I had been thrust into a situation that felt like the same thing all over again. And I couldn't help but wonder: Why do I always have to be the first? I don't always want to be the first!

Times like these are when I'm especially grateful for my

spiritual beliefs. In those tough moments, life has a way of serving up, it's all about finding a way to surrender. I truly believe that whatever happens in my life, whether it's good or bad, is meant to happen. Everything I go through is supposed to be a line in my book—a line in the story of my life. For the longest time—the first quarter century of my life!—The Knowing was attached to my desire to know what I had: what was wrong with me medically. Now that I have my diagnosis, The Knowing has shifted to being more about knowing what is good for me, so that I can have the strength and willpower to move forward. I know what kind of life I want to build for myself, and I have a strong sense of how to make that happen. For me, at this point in my life, that is The Knowing.

Looking back, I can see how narrow my concept of The Knowing used to be, prediagnosis. It was understandable— I just wanted to know what I had and to be able to put a name to my collection of symptoms! But back then, I never dreamed of how much bigger The Knowing could be.

That must be how it is for all of us. We all face challenges in our lives, and often, they are experiences that we would never opt for if we had the choice. But going through them, as tough as they can be, brings us to new levels of personal depth and understanding that we couldn't have even guessed at before.

That is The Knowing, for all of us.

CHAPTER 10

Don't Judge a Book by Its Cover

Wow—we've just covered a lot of deep, heavy stuff. Let's take a minute now to lighten things up. Let's get really superficial, actually: Let's discuss appearances, vanity, and insecurity.

Recently, I heard about a bookstore in Australia that offers readers a "Blind Date with a Book." These are books that have been chosen by the store's staff members, wrapped in brown paper to mask the cover and delivered to the reader's door. Customers have no way to judge what's inside except by starting to read.

That's such a cool idea! And it's such a great metaphor for what we should do in real life, with other people. We should never judge each other by our covers.

Of course, doing that is hard to avoid. Our looks, our appearance, the face we present to the world—often, that's the first thing other people see about us. That's true in dating, in a job interview, at school, on social media...It's true in almost every aspect of life.

People usually think I'm beyond feeling insecure about my appearance or that I'm above it. After all, I've had a whole lifetime to get used to the way I look, right? But I'm human, aren't I? Most people feel insecure at one time or another, no matter what they look like. And we Americans live in a society and culture that places a huge amount of importance on material things—what we wear, what kind of car we drive, what kind of house we live in, and maybe most of all, what we look like. Unfortunately, that can contribute to a culture of meanness, of judgment, of believing that our self-worth is somehow based on our net worth—our possessions, our income, and all those other things that don't really matter.

Still, even knowing material possessions don't matter, it can be really hard not to get caught up in appearances, even for me. Maybe especially for me. My looks really are rather unique, and being in the public eye adds a layer of complication to the entire issue.

If I weren't famous, of course, I would still be dealing with the same insecurities, but at least one aspect of it might be easier: Handling my problems privately might at least save me from the vulnerability I feel when I post a raw, candid video on YouTube, laying all my feelings bare to the world.

And so many of my emotional moments are ones many people can relate to. Some days, for example, I absolutely hate my body. Okay, I shouldn't even say "some days"—the truth is, at some point every day, I'll feel as if there's something about my body that I hate, and I'll get incredibly frustrated.

Sometimes it's purely superficial—for instance, not liking the way my clothes fit me or wishing I weren't so self-conscious about my legs. Sometimes, it's all I can do to make a joke about it and try to move on.

One year, Jessica and I took Sara to an Ed Sheeran concert for her birthday. That evening brought together two things I normally try to avoid: large crowds and wearing shorts in public. I can't help it—I'm embarrassed of my legs! So normally, shorts are out. That goes double in a crowded place, since crowds can really make me nervous.

That night, I decided to risk both the crowded venue and the dicey fashion choice. It was worth it to me, especially since I was going out with my two closest friends. Still, I had a huge sense of hesitation as I dressed for the evening.

I wore a new outfit—a romper with shorts—and it was really cute, but I could probably have fit my entire body into one of the legs. Still, I went ahead and put it on, even though I wasn't exactly feeling confident.

The concert was at the Frank Erwin Center, a huge entertainment arena in Austin that seats thousands and thousands of people. When we arrived, I took a deep breath. Whenever I'm in a situation like that, I have to mentally prepare myself beforehand—to coach myself: *Okay, this is what we're doing. Just have fun, and if you feel awkward, ignore it.*

As we walked in, Sara asked me, "How many times do you think you'll be recognized?"

I laughed, but inwardly, I was cringing. I felt so self-conscious that the very idea of anyone seeing or approaching me sounded awful! So I tried to blow off the entire possibility. "Oh," I said as casually as I could, "probably, like, two at most."

I was so wrong. Within the first five minutes we were there, four or five people had already come up to us. Thirty minutes in, at the end of the opening act, I basically held an impromptu meet-and-greet. Girls were lining up to say hello as I stood on the stairs, taking pictures with everyone. It was a surreal moment for me. There I was freaking out about something as superficial as wearing shorts, while all these people were coming up to me because they found my story inspiring.

It wasn't long before I forgot all about my legs poking out of my romper! That was a wonderful full-circle moment, to be able to realize, *Wow—I'm not doubting myself right now. I'm having a good time, I'm happy I'm here, and I never knew I'd be able to experience something so simple and fun.*

That night turned out to be a wonderful experience, but my insecurities didn't stay away forever. They always have a way of resurfacing, especially when I'm recognized in public by strangers asking me for a picture. I'll take a photo with a fan and then immediately wonder, *Are my legs showing?* Or, if I'm wearing little booties, *Do my ankles look way too small and my shoes way too big?*

I know I'm not alone in these kinds of worries. Unfortunately, women's outward appearances are closely tied to our sense of self-worth. This is something I'm coming to terms with because I know that I, like everyone else, have so much to offer the world that has nothing to do with my appearance. Still, sometimes I can't help getting caught up in superficial insecurities.

And certain places somehow have the power to make me instantly lose all the self-confidence I've built up over the years. Huge concerts are never easy; the beach is even worse. When I was little, my family and I visited Galveston and Port Aransas several times, along the Texas Gulf Coast. Every time we went, I felt so uncomfortable. My self-confidence would drain out of me the second I stepped onto the sand, because I felt so aware of everyone staring at me. To this day, when I go swimming, I have to coach myself through turning off that self-consciousness so I can focus on enjoying myself.

Who knows? Maybe those thoughts and insecurities will turn out to be something I'll experience my whole life. I hope they'll decrease over time, but I doubt I'll ever just wake up someday and find those worries are gone.

Whenever I see myself onscreen, especially when watching my documentary, I immediately get little butterflies in my stomach. It's not that I don't like what I see; it's more that I have to brace myself each time for the fact that a whole new group of people is getting this intimate view into my life. It's like, *Here's my life—here we go.* Audiences see all my loved ones; they hear all my painful stories; they even see inside my apartment—and for so long, I hid all of that.

I've even found myself in the grip of my insecurities at incredible, once-in-a-lifetime moments and events, such as Geena Davis's inaugural Bentonville Film Festival in 2015. I was so honored to receive the Spirit Award, but as I walked up to the stage to accept this incredible award, all I could think about was that I was wearing a dress and sandals. I was so conscious of whether people might be staring at my legs and my feet, even though that was probably the last thing anyone else in the room was paying attention to.

And if I thought walking onto that stage was tough, walking the runway at a fashion show was even harder!

Yes, you read that right: Last year, I got to model in a fashion show, where I strutted the runway and everything. It was an incredible experience and incredibly surreal. Every time I thought about it—*me*, walking down a fashion runway—it made me laugh. It still does!

Don't get me wrong: I love fashion. I love trying on cute new clothes and shoes and doing my hair, and I like to think I've got some pretty sweet style goin' on. But let's be honest— I don't exactly think of myself as looking anything like a model, and I'm not the daintiest walker in the world.

Most of all, after a lifetime of being stared at in public for all the wrong reasons, it's hard for me to put myself on display for everyone to see. So of course I had mixed feelings about walking the runway, and plenty of anxiety in the days leading up to the show. Every time I thought of it, I almost had a heart attack at the very idea.

The show wasn't just any fashion show. It was called Role Model Runway, and it was put on by the Girls' Lounge as part of South by Southwest (SXSW) 2016—the huge music-and-film festival that happens every March in Austin. The Girls' Lounge is dedicated to supporting and mentoring women to find their voices, embrace their feminine leadership powers, and work together to transform corporate culture for current and future generations. They're all about effecting real, positive change for women, which is right up my alley.

I'd worked with the Girls' Lounge the previous year at SXSW. That year, 2015, a group of girls from the Girls' Lounge presented me with a really cool app they'd made about bullying and self-love, and I'd also gotten to meet Cat Greenleaf. Cat is the host of the USA Network's *Talk Stoop*, a show where she sits on a stoop with her dog, presenting pop culture news and interviewing celebrities. She's interviewed people like Eva Longoria, Michael J. Fox, and LL Cool J, and she does it all with her dog. I absolutely loved meeting her!

The following year, when SXSW rolled around again, the Girls' Lounge contacted me to be a part of their Role Model Runway. When they said I was one of their role models, I felt so honored! When I learned Cat Greenleaf would be involved, I couldn't say no.

However, the idea of walking down a runway seemed bizarre. I loved the idea that I was a role model to people— but a *runway* model? That wasn't exactly something I was comfortable with. I knew I needed to connect with my inner confidence if I wanted to make it a positive experience.

Humor ended up being my path toward confidence, just as it always has been. The fashion show happened shortly after I'd finally gotten the pin removed from my toe after my latest foot surgery, so I started thinking of it as my new foot debut. The thought of that made me laugh—debuting my brand-new, postsurgery foot on the runway. And when I laugh, I can't feel nervous!

When the day of the fashion show finally came, the whole experience was overwhelming in the best way possible. The show was hosted by Stacy London, the style advisor who for many years co-hosted *What Not to Wear*. And "Role Model Runway" was exactly right: I had the honor of walking the runway with a group of truly powerful, intelligent, and inspiring women. We each walked with our designers—the women who had designed the shirts we wore, based on something about us that inspired them.

My designer was Nina Brewster, who is with the Girls' Lounge and who happens to have a philosophy that perfectly matches mine. She is focused on equality and says that change can happen only if we do it together—all of us. What a perfect pairing we were. I loved the shirt she designed for me, which said *Brave Is Beautiful* in sparkly letters. It went perfectly with my BRAVE necklace (which, of course, I wore that day, since I never take it off).

My dad couldn't be there for the show. SXSW always coincides with the week of spring break, and he had traveled to Houston the day of the fashion show for a field trip with his fifth graders to see a stage production of *The Little Mermaid*. (Have I told you my dad is crazy about anything Broadway? *Crazy*. His school trip to Houston might have been even more exciting for him than it was for the kids.)

I understood why he couldn't make it to my show, but I still really wished he could be there. The second I'd told him I'd been invited to walk, he'd burst out laughing. He and I have the same sense of humor, and he saw the same potential for comedy that I did in the idea of my walking down a fashion runway.

Since my dad couldn't be in the audience, I was especially glad my mom and Marina were able to come. They spent the whole day with me—and, of course, my mom cried when I walked down the runway. She cried a lot, apparently. After the show was over, Marina told me, "Before they called you up, she cried. When you walked out, she cried. When you walked back, she cried!"

My mom teared up all over again at that, even though we were laughing at the same time. She hugged me. "I was just so proud! That's why it made me cry."

That's my mom for you. She's the best.

———

My insecurities about my looks definitely didn't come from my family or my friends. Growing up, my family never once made me feel as if I looked strange. In fact, many people in my family don't seem to realize I look different from anyone else! They've known me too long. To them, I just look like me—like Lizzie.

My aunts and uncles are so used to the way I look, not to mention so protective of me, that they get angry when random strangers stare at me in public. My parents and siblings and I are so accustomed to that by now that we hardly even notice it anymore, but my extended family members are uncomfortably aware of every single glance.

Once, when we were all out at a restaurant, one of my aunts asked my mom, "How can you just ignore that? You're acting like it's not even happening!"

When I heard that, my immediate thought was, *Exactly! What are we supposed to do—react to every person who does a double take, or turn every instance into a teachable moment? If* we did that, it would take so long, we'd never get out of the restaurant!

Don't get me wrong: Teachable moments can be incredible opportunities to spread positivity and awareness. But not every snicker or stare is worth the effort. In my mind, what's more meaningful is simply to go on about your business, regardless of whether your physical appearance fits "the norm." Even if you look a little unusual, you're a member of the human race. You get to go out in public, just like anyone else, no matter what you look like!

When I talk about differences and insecurities, I often focus on physical appearance, but I do recognize there are a million other ways in which people can feel "different" or "weird." Whether it's your personality, a diagnosis of some kind, your interests or beliefs, or pretty much anything else about you that happens to fall outside the narrow boundaries of "the norm," it's all too easy to slip into self-doubt.

That's why it's so important to focus on the parts of ourselves that we're proud of—our qualities that we like. There are many aspects of myself that I love, absolutely and unconditionally. I love my sense of humor; I love that I was raised to be able to laugh in any situation, good or bad. That's a quality that has gotten me very, very far. I also love that I am a compassionate person, and I love that I have people in my life who can come to me when they need a friendly ear or a shoulder to cry on. I really appreciate that I get to be that confidante for a lot of people.

And I love my tenacity. When a new idea occurs to me, I can't let it go; I have to pursue it, or it will drive me crazy.

When I set a goal, I can't be satisfied until I find a way to reach it—or at least do my very best so I can honestly say I tried.

Even appreciating all these positive qualities of mine, I still struggle with self-doubt. I know I'm not alone in that. No matter how confident you are, no matter how much work you've done to strengthen yourself from the inside out, it is still so common to go through these little internal struggles.

The good news is, it's also perfectly possible to overcome them and continue living your best life. With the good always comes the bad, in every situation. Living your best life doesn't mean you'll suddenly be perfectly self-assured in every situation and never face another crisis of confidence. The key is just to be gentle with yourself in those vulnerable moments and not let them outshine all the good there is to appreciate about yourself and the world around you.

Despite my many struggles regarding my body, I am so grateful for the fact that my body is the way it is. This is the way I look, and I don't want to apologize for it or change it in any way. Still, several fans have sent me pictures over the years—photographs of me that they've Photoshopped. I know they mean it in the kindest way when they tell me, "This is how you would look if you didn't have a syndrome."

One picture I received was especially striking. I couldn't stop staring at it. The Photoshopping was so well done, it really could have passed as me without this syndrome of mine. The image, and the feelings it produced within me, stuck with me for days. I kept looking at it and thinking about it. Some days, I really liked it. I would think, *This is great—this is so crazy to see what I would look like!* And then, other days,

I would look at it and think, *There is no way I would ever, ever want to look like that. Ever.*

I still don't know whether that's because the way I look has become my own version of "normal" or if it's because of my strong belief that I was made this way for a reason. Why would I want to change something that I believe so deeply was meant to be?

One thing I do know: I will always believe that what's needed in this life and this world is not for me to change to look more like everybody else. The world doesn't need you to change yourself to be more "normal," either. What is "normal," anyway?

What the world needs is more people who truly embrace differences, physical and otherwise. We don't need to "fix" everything about ourselves that makes us unique. Rather, we need to fix this terrible misconception that far too many people seem to have that everyone needs to be exactly the same. Uniqueness is a good thing!

It drives me crazy that we, as a species, are so unevolved in this particular way. How many of us have qualities or features that we pick and poke at relentlessly—aspects of our bodies or our personalities that we hyperfocus on and critique? How many of us tell ourselves we aren't good enough because this certain aspect of who we are is just too weird? Too fat, too thin, too tall, too short, too light, too dark, too quiet, too loud, too...just *too*. How much precious, valuable time has each of us wasted on these terrible, toxic messages of nonacceptance that are, in the end, so pointless and unnecessary?

I am here to tell you: It is fine to be who you are. It is a *good* thing not to be just like everybody else. What makes you unique is what makes you beautiful, because it's what makes you *you*. And the world needs you, exactly as you are. That's the truth, plain and simple.

I am very aware that I should take my own advice. I should never feel unhappy about the way my legs look. Instead of worrying about what size they are, I should simply be grateful I have legs to walk on in the first place. But remembering that can be so hard.

A reminder of that came recently with my mom and my grandma. This is my father's mother, who has diabetes; her doctors had to amputate one of her legs, and she's been in a wheelchair for a long time. Technically, she could walk with a prosthetic leg. My whole family always tells her, "You can do it!" But she always says it's too painful.

I was FaceTiming her recently, and out of the blue, she said, "*Mija*, I want to go on a trip with you, but I can't, because I only have one leg."

My first instinct with my grandma, of course, was to demand, "What are you talking about? You can go anywhere you want with just one leg. You don't need *any* legs to travel!"

She just started laughing. But the irony was plain to me: Just like her, I'd been limiting myself in my own mind, in my own way.

Everyone tortures themselves about something—some aspect of themselves they wish they could change. But you do not deserve that kind of negativity. You are perfect just as you are, and so am I.

CHAPTER 11

The Cape Comes Off

Do you think of yourself as a superhero? Probably not—but you should. Everyone is a superhero! Everyone has a cape hanging in their closet, just waiting for them to decide to put it on. All you have to do is figure out what your superpower is.

If I were a superhero, my superpower would be compassion, and I'd have a sidekick called humor.

Before I go any further, let me say this: I really hope this doesn't come across sounding as if I have a big head. All right—I may have a huge forehead, but I swear, my head as a whole is actually pretty small. I have to buy child-size hats and everything! I once ordered a child-size headband online, and the company sent me a note saying they hoped my "little one" looked adorable in it. Little did they know my "little one" was me!

Some people actually seem to view me as a kind of superhero, which is hugely humbling and a great honor. Of course, it's easy for people in the public eye to come across that way. When someone has millions of fans, people who don't know them can start seeing them as almost larger than life. That's especially true if they never reveal their normal, human side—their worries, their flaws, their shortcomings, and vulnerabilities.

I feel lucky and grateful that my superpower is compassion. I want to help as many people as I can, and I post my YouTube videos and respond to my followers' comments because I really want to connect with them. I want to help them through whatever tough times they might be going through.

A friend of mine once said there was something unique about me—not the unique way I look, but a certain approachable quality she thinks I have. She said there is something genuine and kind about me that shines out when I speak and something in my essence that people just respond to.

When I finished blushing at her compliment, I wondered if part of that quality she was talking about might actually be my resilience—the fact that no matter what happens, no matter what's thrown at me, I won't back down. The more negativity I encounter, the more I'll keep fighting. The more challenges pop up in my path, the more determined I am to push through them and keep going. I won't stop! My work is so far from done. I'm more recognizable out on the street now than ever before in my life, but that doesn't mean I'm finished. I haven't reached some plateau where I can just sit back, relax, and take a deep breath. If something terrible were to happen to me tomorrow, I couldn't use it as an excuse to stop what I'm doing. I have to keep going, keep pushing, because there are still people out there who need help, who need to know they are loved and accepted for exactly who they are. And I want to give that to them—and to you in these pages. I want to help people everywhere find that love and acceptance within themselves, so they can give it out to others as well.

My friend might think there's something unique about me, but the truth is that there's something unique about each and every one of us. Everyone has a superpower of one kind or another. Your superpower might be your intelligence, your sharp wit, or your mad basketball skills. It might be your incredible singing voice, your ability to write poetry that moves people, or the wonderful hugs you give to the people you love the most.

Here's one more truth: I am definitely *not* a superhero. If I ever forget that, my body is sure to remind me on a regular basis. Dealing with various health issues is my reality. Doctor's appointments, blood tests, hospital stays—you name it, I've done it over the years. (Maybe even over the past week.)

That can cause problems with my demanding professional life. Sometimes I have to fit major surgeries into the few blank slots left in my speaking schedule. Even keeping up with producing new short videos for my YouTube channel can be tricky when I'm dealing with a health issue. But my job is to inspire people to be their best, most compassionate selves, and I take that job very seriously. That's why I always try to bring it when I go on camera or onstage.

Every time I go onstage for an event, something happens that strikes me as almost magical. No matter how good or bad my health has been leading up to the event, suddenly, for that hour or so that I'm under those bright lights, in front of an audience and with a job to do, something comes over me.

Maybe it's connected to my BRAVE necklace—maybe that necklace is my lucky charm, my own personal talisman that helps me stay strong even when I'm feeling weak.

Sara thinks it's something more spiritual than that. She has described it as something big that shows up to get me into the best shape possible, so I can deliver for my audience, my cause, and my mission.

Whatever it is, the second I get offstage, my human body returns. It happens every time: The cape comes off.

I'm not a superhero after all. I'm just me, Lizzie, a human being in a rather tiny and vulnerable body.

———

During my trip to Malaysia in 2015, when I spoke at the National Achievers Congress, my cape came off in a big way. I had the enormous honor of being one of the first two women ever to headline the event—but I could hardly even breathe during my speech. I was just so sick! At one point, not even ten minutes before I was due to go onstage, I had to lie down on the couch, close my eyes, and pray: *Please, help me get through this somehow.* I even lost my voice at one point during my speech, but somehow I managed to get through it. There was my magic cape, hard at work for me once again.

That magical *something* isn't restricted to my speaking engagements. It happens at other times, too—whenever I need to show up and "bring it" for an audience or an event. During the 2015 SXSW film festival, the year *A Brave Heart* premiered, we were incredibly busy with interviews, meetings with the press, and interacting with audience members. One day, after hours of functioning as Onstage Lizzie, we got into the car to head home.

As soon as I buckled my seat belt, I slumped forward and put my head in my lap. My mom started rubbing my back.

Chris, my little brother, was in the car with us. I guess my sudden shift from Superhero Lizzie to No Cape Lizzie alarmed him because he sounded upset when he asked, "What are you doing? What's wrong?"

My mom told him, simply, "This is what she does."

My mom knows from experience how important it is to acknowledge limitations, and she knows we can't be superheroes all the time. That particular day, she knew I'd been wearing my cape while I needed its strength, and then, as soon as I didn't need it anymore, it came off.

Whenever I have to do something big, my body goes on autopilot. I love that—that magical *something*. Whatever it is, it's a true gift, and I am so grateful for it, because I can always count on it. It has never let me down. But sometimes, when the event is over and my cape comes off, being thrust back into the reality of my human body really isn't any fun.

When I attended the briefing in Washington, D.C., where we spoke to lawmakers about the antibullying bill that we hope will someday be passed, I was incredibly sick. That trip had come at the tail end of several others: After traveling to San Diego, I had then visited Los Angeles, North Carolina, and Mexico City— one flight after another, one city after another, with only a day or two spent in each place. D.C. was our last stop, and without warning, as soon as we arrived, I suddenly felt more ill than I'd felt in a long time. My body hit a wall, at the worst time possible.

The day of the briefing, I stayed in bed as much as I could. Someone did my hair while I was sleeping, and my mom did my makeup. I only got up to do the briefing. The cape really came off quickly that day. I'm not even convinced it was ever fully on.

That superhero cape coming off isn't just a physical thing. It can also be an emotional phenomenon or a combination of the two. Though my parents and I are used to dealing with my ongoing health issues, they can still cause us lots of stress. When I have an important appointment coming up, such as a scheduled surgery or a checkup with my cardiologist, my mom will post it on the calendar at my parents' house so everyone in the family knows what I'm doing. They all know how nervous those appointments can make me feel. They know the state I go into. Until the appointment is behind me, it's at the forefront of my mind, where it crowds out anything and everything else. The anticipation is the worst part! Whether it's as routine as a checkup or as major as a surgery, I never know what's going to happen or what the results are going to be until I go through it, and that is so tough.

I have good reason to feel that way. I've had too many experiences with the unexpected popping up during a routine appointment. During one cardiology checkup, for example, I was shocked to find out I had a back problem. Not long after that, I wound up in the hospital with esophagitis—painful ulcers in my throat—for the second time in two years. As if the ulcers themselves weren't painful enough, that hospital visit resulted in an enormous insurance snafu when it turned out I couldn't see my own, regular doctor. That was a huge issue for me. I've been with the same doctors since I was a baby, and I can't stand starting over with someone new. My medical charts aren't like a regular person's—just a manila folder with some pages in it. Mine are literally in volumes. Visiting an unfamiliar doctor is a huge deal!

Considering my ongoing health issues, it may sound odd that I always think of my body as being pretty strong. But think about it: It's been through so much, and yet, it's still going! At the same time, I can't deny that my body is also vulnerable. When I get sick, the cape comes off pretty quickly—and it's only more pronounced when there's fear or anxiety involved.

Those emotionally charged situations are the ones I really have to watch out for. The physical health stuff is straightforward: I get sick, I have to go to the doctor or maybe the hospital, and then I get better. The emotional stuff is far more subtle. Weird things can happen inside my head that I don't even notice until they've already grown enormous.

Does that ever happen to you? It's like when you stare at a common word for so long that you start wondering, *Is that even spelled right?* When you dwell on something for too long, it can grow way out of proportion in your mind and become like the monsters children fear when they're alone in their dark room at night. If you turn on the light and shine it into those shadowy corners, you'll see there was never really anything there to fear—but that's easier to say than it is to do.

———

Superheroes come into their powers at different times and in different ways. A young girl named Adalia Rose who lives here in Austin is a superhero to me. She has a condition called progeria, which is a genetic disorder that causes rapid aging. One morning, I saw Adalia and her mother featured on the local news, talking about their efforts to raise funding for progeria research. Instantly, I felt drawn to that sweet girl, so I put out a call on Twitter to try to connect with her. Within two hours, a family friend had reached out and put us in contact.

Her mother invited me to come over and meet Adalia. My sister and a friend accompanied me to their house, and as soon as we walked into her toy room, Adalia sat me down and started doing my makeup with her sweet, tiny hands.

I loved her so much! I made a video of our day for my YouTube channel and titled it "Big Things in Small Packages." From the first moment I'd seen her on TV, Adalia Rose struck me as a superhero. She was so small, yet she was one of the strongest people I had ever met. Her superpower was definitely her inner strength—and I was so excited to learn she had the same superhero sidekick as mine: humor. She kept me laughing the entire time we were together.

Her mom turned on music at one point during our visit, and Adalia started dancing like nobody was watching. She shook her little hips like there was no tomorrow! She was owning it—living her best life in the body she was born with.

Every single one of us has a superhero cape hanging in the closet, just waiting for us to take it out and try it on. All you have to do is decide when you're ready to handle the responsibilities that come with it. And that can be a weighty thing. Believe me, I know. Making the decision to be strong and brave, when those are the last things you feel inside—that isn't easy.

Here's the exciting part, though: You get to decide what your superpower will be. Is it compassion, like mine? Is it laughter, like Megan Meier's? Is it strength, like Adalia Rose's? Or is it something else altogether? Only you can decide, since you know yourself best.

Whatever your superpower is, I know it's something incredible that will be a true gift to the world, as soon as you decide to pull that cape out of your closet and try it on.

CHAPTER 12

The Truth About Strength

My superhero cape has certainly come off in some epic ways. In those moments, I have had to dig deep to access my own inner strength. But sometimes, all I can do is simply admit that I need help.

When I've found the strength and courage to do that, I have been filled with gratitude for the people who have come to my aid in countless ways, both large and small. My family, friends, and fans—so many people in my life have held me up when I might otherwise have collapsed, sometimes in a very literal sense. That aspect of vulnerability is beautiful. The irony, of course, is that vulnerability has become a huge part of how I define true strength.

Being truly strong includes not always having to pretend you are strong. I've learned that it takes real courage to let yourself be vulnerable in front of other people and ask for help. Finding the courage within ourselves to be vulnerable is a big part of the sea change I am calling for—the cultural shift toward greater kindness and compassion, for ourselves as well as for others, that is so very needed right now. You need to be open and honest with others about the experiences you've had that have hurt you and to be humble enough to ask for help, if and when you need it.

I know that isn't easy. Believe me, I know! But whatever you have gone through, I guarantee you aren't the only one. There are other people out there experiencing the same things. If you open up about your feelings, you'll find your tribe—the people who understand and support you and who will be so grateful for your help and support in their own lives. We are all in this together, right?

I am living proof that this is true. Look at me: I have an extremely rare genetic condition that only a handful of other people have. I have been bullied my entire life, online and in person. Yet my insecurities aren't that different from anyone else's. When I started being more open and vulnerable, it spurred an incredible community of support that continues to amaze me every day. I have found my tribe.

You can find your tribe, too.

———————

Allow me to be blunt: The consequences of *not* finding the courage to be vulnerable are dire. If you always keep your true feelings and your inner wounds to yourself, the best that can result is emotional isolation from everyone around you, even the people who love you the most. That's just the way it works.

That's not the only thing you risk if you refuse to be open and vulnerable. You also risk experiencing a breakdown, like

I did, one that results from a constant building of inner tension that escalates to the point of exploding. Or, even worse, you risk becoming a hurt person who hurts other people due to your own inner pain—in short, a bully.

That sounds harsh, but I don't know any other way to address it except directly. People consider me something of an unofficial authority on bullies and bullying, and I think I can say this with some certainty: Pain and anger have to go somewhere. If we keep stuffing them down instead of processing them, we'll end up either turning them inward, which isn't good, or outward, which is no better.

———

Bullying, in essence, is an individual's inner pain turned outward and directed at someone else. That's just one unfortunate facet of human nature, and it happens all over the world. That's why bullying is a global phenomenon. Think about the bullies you encounter on a daily basis, even those whose anger isn't directed at you. It seems like everyone knows someone who's always on a power trip or constantly in some fit of rage.

You may not think of those people as bullies, but in essence, that's what they are. Bullying crosses race, gender, culture, and class lines, and it has happened throughout the history of our species. Yet many people seem to think bullying only happens among children and that it's caused by factors as simple as what kids see at home, at school, and in the media.

Those are not the only answers to why bullying occurs. Even more than that, pointing fingers in that particular way feels uncomfortably close to a blame-someone-else mentality.

In the end, asking why bullying occurs may not necessarily be the most important question. Perhaps we would do better to focus on how best to respond to bullies, in order to create a better outcome for everyone involved.

That makes compassion for the bully crucial, but it is incredibly difficult for a bullying victim to feel empathy for the person who has caused them pain. When you are being taunted or shamed, when you're being excluded or called hurtful names, when you're the subject of awful rumors—when you're being hurt by someone physically, mentally, or emotionally, over and over again, it is next to impossible to view your tormentor with compassion. The likelihood that their bullying is resonating from some profound wound within themselves is probably the last thing on your mind.

Let's face it: In order to feel compassion for a bully, you have to be able to shrug it off when they spew out their hate at you.

It is an enormous understatement to say that isn't easy to do. It's taken me a long time to learn to do it myself.

Recently, someone left a comment on my YouTube channel that said, "Why is everyone lying to Lizzie, telling her she's pretty? We all know she isn't pretty. SHE knows she isn't pretty. I may be rude, but at least I'm not a liar."

In the past, I might have ignored that comment or relied on my fans to address it among themselves. But I've been trying to walk the talk, so to speak, and live by my own advice—so I went ahead and addressed the comment directly with one of my own:

"We each have our own perspective," I wrote, "and that's great. I respect your opinion. But there's a way to voice it that isn't so blunt. Thanks for your comment, I hope you have a great day!"

Their response to mine came within moments, and it amazed me: "Wow, it's really you!! I'm a huge supporter of yours!!"

I was floored. My technique had worked! Instead of just ignoring that commenter or shrugging them off as a troll, I reached out to them directly, with compassion and respect, and they responded back with a message of support to let me know they were in my corner.

Responding with compassion simply isn't the intuitive reaction when someone lashes out to hurt us. Anger, fear, or turning the negativity inward—these are far more typical reactions.

Why is that? What is it about human nature that makes us assume we deserve it when someone lashes out at us? I am no psychologist, so I really don't know the answer. But just think about it: When you get twenty sincere compliments and just one nasty criticism, which is the comment that's going to stick with you? For a lot of us, it's that one, single criticism that we're most ready to believe. It's the one we'll allow to sink into our subconscious and take root, where it feeds our doubts and insecurities about being unworthy of love, acceptance, and respect.

For far too many of us, of course, it's not as simple as one criticism among a sea of compliments causing lasting emotional damage. Often, the reason that single criticism can root so deeply is that it's building on a foundation of inner wounds sustained from early childhood on. People undergo all kinds of negative experiences at home, at school, and among friends—events both insidious and traumatic that can leave them feeling as if the world is an unsafe and unstable place.

A single nasty comment is not the same thing as bullying. Bullying is ongoing, systematic, and intentional; that's what makes it so damaging. The fact that it often happens in childhood only makes it worse. There is something about childhood experiences that can affect us much more deeply, and for a much longer time, than the experiences we undergo once we're older. For a child to be bullied carries a profoundly heavy emotional impact.

Still, I can't help but wonder about issues of emotional damage and resiliency. Having Ollie in my life adds context to my wonderings. See, Ollie does silly stuff sometimes. (Okay, he does silly stuff a lot!) He might destroy a brand-new toy in about five minutes flat, or bark too much, or poop on my carpet. When he does those things, I get frustrated with him. But does my frustration cancel out the love I give him all day long? Of course not! He's a smart dog; he understands perfectly well when he's done something wrong. He might hang his head for a moment, to show me he gets it. Then he goes right back to grinning and wagging his tail, and he's ready to jump into my lap for a cuddle as soon as I call his name. He's that quick and easy to forgive.

I wish I could be more like Ollie, shaking things off that easily and getting right back to the love instead of dwelling in the hurt. Why is it so hard to be forgiving and emotionally resilient? It takes a lot to break a dog's spirit, but humans? One crummy comment can ruin our whole day, and one uncaring person in our lives can leave us feeling broken inside.

Over time, I have developed a process for protecting myself from the negativity I encounter in the world. This might include stories in the news that bring me down, an argument with a friend, or negative comments I encounter on social media. Whatever the source of the negativity might be, my game plan is to actively isolate it from myself—from my own values, beliefs, and perspective. To me, this is a sorting process—separating the good from the bad—and I approach it in a very aware and deliberate way. If someone says something to me that could hurt my feelings, for example, I acknowledge to myself how they feel, but remind myself that I don't have to agree, and I don't have to take their criticism to heart. I believe in my own truth; I define myself.

I have also come to realize, though, that there is a definite positive side to our emotional fragility. It's not all about isolating ourselves from negativity; there's also a lot of beauty and strength in allowing ourselves to be open and vulnerable. We are here to help each other. That, in my mind, is our purpose as a species. It's the whole point of being human: to love ourselves and each other and do it better every day if possible. So it follows that we are also emotionally fragile. Otherwise, we wouldn't need to help each other at all.

Imagine if each and every one of us, every single person on Earth, had enough wisdom, confidence, and self-acceptance to be able to say to a bully, "I understand that how you're treating me has nothing to do with me. It's a reflection of how you feel inside, and I want to help you. What's happening in your life? How can I help?"

If we were able to do that instantly, naturally, and

instinctively, we wouldn't even need to help each other. We would all be just fine!

There is something very spiritual about that to me—about our need to be there for one another and give one another the gift of our understanding and compassion.

———

Finding forgiveness can be a tall order. It can be difficult to forgive others if we've gone through an immense amount of hurt. After all, in order to love others, we must love ourselves first. But if we come from an abusive or neglectful background, loving ourselves may not come easily. Our feelings of unworthiness can run incredibly deep, and nothing anyone says or does can touch that wounded inner core that won't believe we could possibly deserve to be loved.

There is, however, a way out of that damage. The path to loving ourselves is through acknowledging our wounds and talking out our feelings to process and understand them. In order to move from a broken place to a place of wholeness, we first have to accept whatever part of ourselves feels broken and own it. That requires being vulnerable and honest about it, first with ourselves and then with other people.

A time when asking for help really made a difference in my life was during my twenty-sixth birthday. It was a pretty hectic week, both personally and professionally—not only was it my birthday, but we were also in the middle of the premiere of our documentary, and I was a headliner at a major event in Austin. To put it lightly, I felt a little mentally undone.

Everywhere we went that week, we had an entourage. We

were so busy that someone from our team would walk with me, holding my grilled cheese and fries so I could walk, eat, and talk to our publicist all at the same time. I remember thinking, *Just tell me where I need to be and what I'm doing next, and I'll do it.*

When my doctor heard about my schedule, he said I was overdoing it. But I knew I could handle it.

Everything went so well that week, and I felt so happy with how things were turning out, that I decided to make an appointment to see my doctor on my own. I had never gone to a doctor's appointment alone before; in the past, one or both of my parents had always gone with me. Going on my own was a huge step in my growing independence, and one that was a long time in coming.

Later, I actually felt a little silly. There I was, a full-grown adult, doing a happy dance because I'd gone to see my own doctor by myself. But for me, it was a big deal! Looking back at that moment, I still feel proud of myself for taking that step.

That whole day was a lot like ripping off a Band-Aid. I knew I would eventually have to start taking charge of my own health and medical appointments, so I finally just did it. There was no particular reason why that was the day; there are just times when I'm very spontaneous about doing things that scare me, and that was one of those days. I was feeling brave, so I took the leap, made the appointment with my doctor, and figured out my own transportation to get to his office.

Once I was there, I took another important leap in building my strength and independence: Since I was alone with my doctor for the first time, I took the opportunity to have a long, open conversation with him about everything that had happened with my breakdown and everything that was going on for me professionally. I told him my anxiety was still sky-high but that medication was out of the question.

My doctor was wonderful about it. He made me feel comfortable, safe, and understood. He also told me we could find a medication that would work for me—something non-habit-forming, in the lowest dose possible that would help relax me instead of knocking me out, the way the previous medication had done.

The appointment went really well. I'd proven to myself that I could manage getting there on time and in one piece, and once there, I'd found the courage to talk with my doctor about a scary personal issue.

That day, I took another step forward in trusting myself. My doctor visit helped me see that I was more than capable of taking care of myself. Part of my personal journey toward true strength came through recognizing both my limitations and my capabilities. I needed help, so I asked for it, and I received it.

Needing help isn't weak. *I* am not weak. I'm a lot stronger than I sometimes think I am, and I'm willing to bet the same is true for you. Most of us aren't fully in touch with our own inner strength. But sometimes we're able to connect with it, or at least get a little glimpse of it when we need it most. If I can do it, I know you can do it, too.

CHAPTER 13

Faith, God, the Universe, and Weird Miracles

Faith is an important concept in our culture. Everyone, regardless of their particular religious beliefs, has the potential to tap into an inner sense of faith and trust in their path. Of course, it can be difficult for some to shine a light on it, but that light seems to have a way of turning on when it's the right time. Or, if you're stubborn like me, you do what it takes to turn it on yourself!

Prayer has played an astounding role in my life, and it has opened me up to incredible wells of inner strength that I can always rely on when I need to. A recent experience with prayer really floored me. It came about when my friend Kamari Copeland texted me on a Sunday morning and asked if there was anything I needed prayer for.

The way Kamari first came into my life is a true example of serendipity. I met her in 2014 through her best friend, the amazingly talented singer Tori Kelly, at that year's SXSW music conference.

Alexis Jones, our executive producer for the documentary, knew I was a huge fan of Tori's, so she reached out to her friend Scooter Braun, who was putting on a showcase of his artists. Never in a million years would I have thought I would get the chance to meet Tori in person. Even just attending her live show at the music festival was a dream! But there I was, getting to see her play live and then actually meeting her backstage. It was an incredible night. I was on cloud nine the entire evening.

The next day, Tori texted me and asked me to attend her show that night, too. At the venue that evening, I hung out backstage with her and Kamari, and we made a real connection as we talked, laughed, and shared our stories. Those two women are both very faith-based, which just impressed me so much.

That evening, Tori surprised me by playing an original song she had written that had been inspired by my TEDx talk. I couldn't believe it. One of my favorite singer-songwriters, a woman whose music, intelligence, and values I admired so very much, had written a gorgeous song inspired by *me*!

I just. Could. Not. Believe it.

Tori and I have kept up our friendship ever since, and Kamari and I have really become close as well.

A couple of years into our friendship, Kamari and I began texting off and on about prayer. I shared with her that I'd been in an odd space for a while, spiritually—that I wanted to dive into my faith in a different way, but I didn't know how or what that different path might be. It was something that had really been on my heart, and the simple act of sharing it with a friend really helped.

Then, one Sunday morning, Kamari texted me out of the blue:

"Just thinking about you. Hope you're having a good day. Is there anything you need prayer for?"

It had been a very emotional weekend for me. I was home between travels for speaking engagements, and, as I've mentioned, downtime can be tricky for me. I'd also been dealing with pain from another recent surgery, and Ollie had been staying with my parents again while I recuperated. I missed him and really wanted him back home with me, and I felt adrift in so many ways.

So I texted Kamari back: "Thank you—I so needed this. My prayer would be for patience."

Even as I texted those words, I knew that everything was in God's timing. Whether it was my health, my love life, my career—no matter what it might be, I knew I needed to have the patience to be able to take a deep breath and say to myself, *It's okay.*

It's all in his timing. I believe that deeply. Yet sometimes, I still get so frustrated and impatient.

Kamari replied with a long text. It was a devotional she had read that morning, and it happened to be about patience.

Reading it, every word gave me chills. It reaffirmed what I had been trying and failing to remember: to be patient and have faith that everything in my life will happen in God's timing.

I may sometimes lose sight of that deep-rooted faith, but it's always there within me, ready for me to access it whenever I am ready to focus within and find it once again.

The same is true for my inner strength. Maybe the two—faith and strength—are really one and the same.

————

What do you have faith in?

That's a big question, but it's an incredibly important one to consider. What keeps you going? What is your greater purpose? What are you here to accomplish for the greater good—what contribution will you make to help this world become a better place?

This rare genetic condition of mine has made it clear to me that we've all been given special gifts, and our purpose is to share them with each other. Having my gift has allowed me to experience things that have taught me humility, strength, and empathy. It has allowed me to spread a powerful message of kindness and self-acceptance to people across the world. What a gift I've been given! It's an incredible gift from the universe.

My syndrome is the larger gift, but I also feel that I receive gifts on a daily basis from God. They come often, and in a variety of ways. Sometimes I receive the exact message I need, right when I need it—a bolt of clarity, a moment of awareness that feels supercharged in my mind. Something will happen, and I'll suddenly be aware: *This is something I need to pay attention to.* Call these moments what you will—synchronicity, messages from God, or gifts from the universe—but they happen to me a lot, and they've happened all my life.

Maybe they happen to you, too. Do things ever just seem to *click* in your life, in a truly magical way? For me, sometimes it feels as if some part of my life has been written in bold print and gone over with a highlighter, to make absolutely sure I'll pay special attention.

One of those experiences for me was in 2015, when I was invited to visit the YouTube headquarters in Los Angeles. They asked me to attend their weekly meeting with the team that works on the site's comments section. Susan Wojcicki, the CEO of YouTube, invited me onstage with her during their meeting, to offer my ideas and opinions about how to reduce the number of terrible, negative, hurtful comments people so often post on others' videos.

To have that input with the very company that had launched it all for me—back when I was seventeen years old and stumbled upon the YouTube video of "The World's Ugliest Woman"—was such a full-circle moment for me. It was so emotional. I was crying; everyone in the meeting was crying. At the end of my visit, they told me, "This isn't just a one-time thing. We value your opinion." To be able to contribute and be valued in that way meant so much to me.

That day lives in my mind as a gift from God. Sometimes he tells me exactly what I need, right when I need it most. And he told me that day that he had given me this syndrome for a higher purpose.

Another time when I experienced a similar message from God was the day I bought a prayer box before my first date with a new guy. I was feeling so nervous that whole day! I knew a prayer box would help me quiet and focus my mind.

Prayer boxes are wonderful: They often come with an inspiring quote on the lid, and they contain paper for you to write down a prayer, a worry, or a bit of Scripture that's on your mind. The idea is to put focus and thought into whatever you write down on the piece of paper, and then, when you put the paper into the box and close the lid, you let it go. You let the worry go; you let the wish or hope go, and you simply *trust*—trust God or the universe to hear your prayer and respond in whatever way is right or meant to be.

Prayer means so much to me, and prayer boxes are incredible. I recommend them for everyone, regardless of your faith or beliefs! It is something everyone can do and benefit from. You can purchase a prayer box, or you can make your own, decorated with quotes or images that mean something special to you. It doesn't really matter what the box is or what it looks like. What matters most is how you use it. The letting-go part is key, because it signals that process of faith and trust in the universe, in God, to hold you and your heart. It signifies faith that you are on the right path or that you are at least approaching it. That's powerful stuff, in my book.

The box I got was so cute—on the top was a quote about "When life gets hard," and inside were the prettiest little papers to write on. The morning that I was nervous about my upcoming date, I wrote the day's date on one of the sheets of paper, and then I wrote down a brief prayer asking for help in just being myself. I put my prayer into the box and closed the lid, and then I did my best to let it go.

All day long, one thing after another happened that just blew me away.

First, I went on my own to another doctor's appointment. I still wasn't used to going to appointments by myself, and once my doctor realized that, he was so proud of me. He said, "You can do this!" Deep down, I've always known I could handle my medical care on my own, but to actually prove to myself that I was more than capable was the best feeling in the world. I felt a little silly taking such pride in something that for most people is routine, but my doctor's encouragement made me see it really was a big deal. I knew I was taking another step in the right direction, toward greater independence.

After the appointment, I took an Uber home, and as I sat in the backseat, I started feeling nervous about my date again. Quickly, though, I was distracted from my worries: Out of the blue, the Uber driver started talking to me about wanting to become a motivational speaker.

Just to be clear, the driver had no idea who I was or what I did for a living. It was just a random encounter.

He told me he loved listening to inspirational podcasts. "I'll play you one," he said, and he started fiddling with buttons on his dashboard.

That made me nervous! I didn't want him to play me some podcast; I wanted him to keep his eyes on the road so he could get me back to my apartment in one piece! While he was busy queuing up the podcast, I kept thinking, *This is so odd—what is he doing?*

The podcast began, and it turned out to be a talk about the importance of authenticity. The speaker said, "All you have to do is be yourself. Just be you, and that's it."

I felt goose bumps start to prickle over my arms. There I

was, in an Uber, listening to this random podcast that turned out to have everything to do with exactly what I'd prayed about that very morning. I've never had that happen before or since, by the way—an Uber driver telling me about his hopes and dreams like that, or playing me one of his favorite podcasts. That struck me as another special message from God, encouraging me to *just be me* on my date. I didn't need to be nervous. I only needed to be me. So simple.

The date went really well, by the way. The guy and I ended up liking each other a lot, and we dated for quite a while. But that experience, that moment of clarity in the Uber, was bigger to me than just the immediate message about my upcoming date or even about my love life in general. To me, that message is one I need to be reminded of every single day because, in essence, it is the very message I am trying to spread to the world. It has everything to do with the issue of bullying, and ultimately, with how we can remedy conflict over our differences in the world.

Think about it: *Just be you.* Isn't that beautifully simple and profound? Think if everyone were able to *just be themselves* and be confident in the fact that, no matter who they are or what they look like, they *are enough*. How incredible would that be? If everyone could do that and know it deeply within themselves, no one would be mean to each other. Everyone would be compassionate toward and accepting of everyone else, in all our weird and wonderful variations.

We aren't quite there yet, as a society. There is still this pervasive idea that we all have to be the same, and any differences among us—in our looks, our cultural backgrounds, our personalities, beliefs, sexual orientations, values—must be hidden or destroyed.

That idea seems to come straight from the media. Consider the way people obsess over celebrities: When it comes down to it, it's *usually* because they happen to appear beautiful. We worship celebrities for many reasons, but it often comes back around to their appearance in some manner. Whether their good looks come through crazy diet and exercise regimens, plastic surgery, or a simple accident of nature, that's what attracts us to them. Celebrity gossip shows, magazines, and websites cash in on this phenomenon. Do they report about celebrities' hard work, their honesty, their kindness, or their charitable works? Sometimes, but not very often. That's not clickbait, and it doesn't sell magazines. Positivity doesn't sell. What does? Pictures of celebrities looking gorgeous—or, worse, pictures of them caught in an off of moment when they look less than perfect. Those might gain even more attention, since they allow "normal" people a moment of feeling superior.

It's no wonder so many of us get caught up in that way of thinking. Celebrity magazines are just one example among many of companies profiting off of human insecurity. Living in the modern world means we can't escape from advertising designed expressly to make us spend money. Have you ever thought about how many of the messages you see on TV, in magazines, and on billboards are designed to make you feel insecure about who you are, so you'll spend money to change yourself in some way? Advertisers want you to feel like you are too fat or too thin, too pimply, too wrinkly, or too cellulite-y; they want you to believe that your hair isn't shiny enough, your car isn't fancy enough, and you definitely aren't sexy enough—but if you eat a certain brand of hamburger or drink a certain kind of beer or buy a certain lotion or drive a certain car, you might just possibly start to be a little thinner/ curvier/less pimply/smoother-skinned/shinier-haired/more desirable/sexier overall.

It's ridiculous! When you really stop and think about it, it is absolutely ridiculous.

Yet as soon as you stop thinking about it quite so directly, those ideas have a sly, sneaky way of worming their way back into your brain. You can't help but absorb those messages; they are everywhere you look. How quickly we forget that being rich can't buy happiness and absolutely no one is perfect—and there's no reason they should be. (And most models' gorgeous, expensive clothes are on loan!)

Speaking of models and weird miracles, a life-changing experience that has enlightened and inspired my work came from an unexpected angel. In early September 2015, I was flattered when Kylie Jenner selected me to be one of the first six people featured in a new antibullying campaign she was launching on Instagram. She posted my picture and tagged it with the campaign's official hashtag, #IAmMoreThan. Almost instantly, the whole thing blew up. Suddenly, outlets like *People* magazine, *Teen Vogue*, and Britain's *Daily Mail* were highlighting my story that Kylie had shared.

To borrow from Kylie's own words about her campaign's message, she shared six stories over the course of six days about "people who have become heroes in their own way by taking #bullying and turning it into something positive."

The pictures Kylie posted and the stories she shared were of people who had been bullied because of something different about them—an illness, a medical diagnosis, a physical disability—but who were defying the odds and overcoming the bullying. She posted a photo of one young woman with a physical disability who was an incredible ballet dancer. She posted another of beauty blogger and retired model Em Ford, who revealed on social media that she had severe acne, and the selfies she posted (without makeup) resulted in more than 100,000 negative comments from followers. Em responded by making a video that went viral, in which she encouraged people to make friends with the person they saw in the mirror. Her video was viewed over 8 million times the first week alone. She really got her positive message out!

On Day 4 of her official campaign, Kylie posted a picture of me. She gave it the caption "#IAmMoreThan the names they call me," and wrote some awesome stuff about me that came straight from her heart. She wrote, "Lizzie taught me #IAmMoreThan who I think I am." That blew me away! It was such an honor that I had inspired Kylie Jenner to view herself in a new, more loving and positive way. At the end of her post, she wrote, "I love you Lizzie! I'll see you soon." That just made my heart so full!

In no time at all, my #IAmMoreThan picture and story were picked up by *Seventeen* and *Cosmopolitan* magazines and several other international outlets—except they focused a lot more on Kylie's story than on mine, especially the fact that she'd taken her Day 4 post as an opportunity to open up and get personal about her anxiety and her own experiences with being bullied online. It really was a big deal, since it was her first time talking so openly about having anxiety. But that became the headline: "Kylie Jenner Admits Anxiety to Bullied Girl!" or "Kylie Jenner Helps World's Ugliest Woman!"

When she first called me to tell me about her campaign, we didn't know each other at all. But just a few minutes into the conversation, we were talking comfortably, like old friends. I shared some details with her about what I'd gone through and what I'm doing now as an antibullying activist. Then the conversation shifted to negative things people post on social media.

When she brought up the mean comments that have been posted about me online, I kind of shrugged it off. "Yeah, I do get plenty of those," I said, "but I'm sure it's nothing close to what you get."

She stopped me pretty quickly. "No," she said, "it's not like that. It's not whether you or I have it worse. Those words hurt us the same way."

I'll admit that stunned me at first. I was taken aback. But very quickly, I realized she was exactly right. I might be looking at her as if she and I were living in two completely different stratospheres—I mean, *Kylie Jenner!* She's gorgeous, she comes from an incredibly famous family, she's on newsstands and TV and all over the Internet, and she lives the Hollywood lifestyle all day, every day. She and I could not be more different. At least, that was what I thought.

Yet she had seen through that superficial stuff a lot faster than I had, to the truth underneath: that just like everyone else on the planet, she and I were the same. We were both people with hearts and feelings, insecurities and vulnerabilities. When random strangers on the Internet said cruel stuff about us, it hurt us both the same. That was a very profound realization, for me, despite the fact that it was tied so closely to what I am always striving for everyone to understand— that we are all the same, we are all in this together, and we all deserve kindness, love, and respect.

I told Kylie about my TEDx talk, and then the conversation turned to my documentary. Kylie said she'd like to see it.

As soon as she said it, I thought how cool it would be if she saw my movie. Immediately, of course, I assumed she wouldn't actually be able to attend one of our upcoming screenings. The woman is probably even busier than I am. Still, I was honored that she'd expressed interest in wanting to watch my film.

A week or two later, she reached out again to say she wanted to attend our Los Angeles screening. I was floored and incredibly flattered, and of course I told her she was welcome to come. Yet I still didn't really believe she'd show up! Maybe that's a defense mechanism of mine: Whenever I'm really excited for something, I always have that thought in the back of my mind that it might not play out the way I hope.

The night of our LA screening, my mom and I rode to the theater with Jess and her boyfriend. We'd all flown in that morning from our New York premiere, so we were very excited but also very sleepy. Honestly, the idea that Kylie might attend our screening wasn't even on my mind.

We walked into the gorgeous theater and took photos in front of the marquee with the movie title on it. In true Lizzie fashion, we also went to the bar and ordered a grilled cheese! Some sweet fans asked for photos while we waited for the screening to begin, and of course I obliged. I love it when I'm able to meet my supporters and chat with them in person.

About a half hour into the movie, my publicist leaned over and told me Kylie had arrived. Instantly, I got the biggest smile on my face! I'll also admit I had butterflies in my stomach as I went out to meet her. She greeted me with a big hug, and we talked outside the theater for a few minutes—after a few much-needed selfies, of course!

When we went into the darkened theater to find our seats, we happened to walk in right at the scene in the film when I'm making a YouTube video with my dad. It's a funny scene, so I was laughing—but then I looked over at Kylie, and I was shocked to see she was crying! Tears were streaming down her face, lit up silver in the light from the movie screen.

Instantly, I was reminded all over again that she's human. This gorgeous woman whose face you can see on newsstands pretty much any day of the week, who grew up "in the business," so you might think she would be hardened or at least used to anything and everything that might get thrown her way—in the end, she's just human, just like anyone else. She has real feelings and a deep and genuine heart.

I'm so glad I was able to meet someone like Kylie. The fact that we've both been the targets of bullying and of other people's mean comments and judgments allowed us to make a very simple and natural connection.

I got to interact with Kylie again a few weeks later, when we launched my #ImWithLizzie campaign in honor of National

Bullying Prevention Month. Kylie took part in the campaign, along with Tori Kelly, America Ferrera, Dr. Oz, Kristen Bell, Zachary Quinto, and many others. A lot of people were involved, and a lot of big names pledged that they were "with Lizzie." Talk about a full heart!

Since then, I've been so glad to see that Kylie has continued with her own antibullying campaign. Initially, she had conceived of it as just a six-day thing, to spotlight six different people whose stories she found inspiring. But after she and I met in LA, she told me that a lot of other people had started using the #IAmMoreThan hashtag. It had taken off, and people were using it to tell some incredibly inspiring stories. Kylie said she wanted to continue doing it on her own platform, since she could reach so many people. And she's really stuck with it! She posts photos sometimes or reposts people's stories that she really connects with.

I'm so impressed with what Kylie Jenner is doing. She's transcending what is normally expected of celebrities, moving beyond her gorgeous good looks by using her platform and her reach to spread a message of positivity that is just wonderful. She is part of the movement to change our culture—to inspire people to be kinder, first to themselves and then to everyone around them.

———

My own antibullying activism is ongoing. I haven't yet accomplished all my goals, and there is still so much to be done. But I have helped to create some significant change, and I've also experienced some incredible gifts and blessings along the way.

When I traveled to D.C. in 2015, I was invited to meet

with House minority leader Nancy Pelosi. That was huge to me. I can hardly put it into words, except to say that I kept wondering if I was awake—if this was really happening.

A year earlier, when we had traveled to D.C. with Tina Meier to visit with people on Capitol Hill and tell our stories in hopes of inspiring them to support the Safe Schools Improvement Act, we'd practically had to beg for meetings.

The next year, we were being *invited* to meetings. I took a picture with Congresswoman Pelosi, which she and I both posted to social media, and it made headlines. It was such an incredible honor—truly one of the weirdest miracles of my life.

Miracles like that have happened throughout my life, and they always amaze me. I have faith that they are gifts from the universe, delivered to me with perfect timing each and every time.

Think about your own life. When have you experienced those bolts of clarity or awareness, those moments of perfect serendipity—when exactly what you needed dropped right into your lap, exactly when you needed it most?

I hope that when you experience those gifts, you take note of them and feel gratitude for their presence in your life. They are truly miraculous!

And if you really focus on the messages you receive during these moments—the feelings you experience and the meaning behind them—it can give you a window into your life's purpose.

CHAPTER 14

The Right Kind of Selfish

As we reflect on empowering ourselves to make the world a better place, here's a truth everyone can probably relate to: Before we can take care of anyone or anything else in our lives, we all need to take care of ourselves a little more. I would even go so far as to say we need to learn how to be selfish —the *right* kind of selfish.

Selfishness can be defined in so many different ways, some good and some definitely not so good. Our families are the first people to define words for us, and it seems like a lot of people misconstrue self-care as selfishness. It's easy to do. We put so much pressure on ourselves to be there for our families and friends, to be *on* all the time for our work, and to be available to anyone or anything depending on us. That's a lot to live up to! I know I have a lot on my plate every second of every day, and I'll bet you do, too. I'll bet there are plenty of people in your life who matter to you, who mean the world to you, and who depend on you every day. That's life, and that's why it's so easy to shift ourselves to the bottom of our own VIP lists.

We all keep VIP lists in our heads—the people who matter most to us, the friends and family members whom we prioritize above all else. These are the people we would do anything for, including dropping everything to care for them if they needed it. But I would venture to guess that very few of us view ourselves in that same protective light. Most of us would do whatever it took to care for others even as we ignored and neglected our own needs, letting stress mount until we reach a breaking point.

This has everything to do with being people-pleasers and perfectionists. Many of us strive to be all things to all people, and that can lead us to neglect ourselves in our drive to please everyone around us.

That's a dynamic that is entirely too familiar to me.

Recently, a friend asked me whether I ever get to be selfish. She meant it in a caring way, as in, *Do you ever make the time to slow down a little and take care of yourself, maybe even pamper yourself a little?* She asked because she sees how hard I push myself, every day, to live up to the demands of my daily life. She sees my travel schedule, my interactions with my fans, both online and in person, and the health issues I deal with on a regular basis. The truth is that certain aspects of my health could be improved if I slowed down a little more often.

That's easier said than done. Because of my busy schedule, which is often planned months in advance with very little wiggle room or downtime, slowing down takes planning and effort. When I do manage some downtime, I always feel guilty about it. The way I see it, that's time I could be using to do something more important. I could be working or trying to help someone in some way. I don't need to relax and focus on myself; I need to be out there, helping as many people as I can in whatever way I can! At least, that's my habitual mind-set. It's one I learned from my dad, and I very much respect that quality in him—that urge to help others whenever possible, in any way he can. I want to be like him in that way, and I strive to live up to his example every day.

Over time, though, I've learned that in order to keep going strong, I have to take care of myself. And doing that has meant getting over my negative associations with the concept of "selfishness," so I can tap into the difference between selfishness and self-care. If I'm not in fighting shape, I can't meet the needs of anyone else depending on me.

That's why, when my friend asked if I ever get to be selfish, I found myself wondering what selfishness actually was. Did I even want to be selfish? Could there be a positive side to it that I'd never considered?

I'd always thought of selfishness as an undesirable character trait. People who are selfish are big-headed. They're self-absorbed. Self-involved. Quick to focus on their own problems, needs, and feelings instead of on the bigger picture. Too often, they put themselves first instead of considering the greater good.

None of that is anything like what I aspire to be. Besides, if I ever started getting a swollen head, my family would be right there to bring me back to reality. I'm so grateful to them for helping me stay grounded!

Those aren't the only definitions of selfishness, how-ever. I'm starting to learn that there are also many positive aspects of selfishness, including self-care and being able to say no—and even, yes, a little pampering from time to time. I'm definitely a work in progress in this area. Allowing myself to relax, to say no, to pamper myself—each of these are things I aspire to get better at, because they're incredibly important aspects of learning to be the *right* kind of selfish.

Back in 2012, I appeared on the TV show *The Doctors* with one of my best friends, Angelica, talking about my then-undiagnosed syndrome. It was a great experience, yet, four years later, when I was invited to appear on the show again, I ended up declining the invitation. That was really tough for me to do. When I'm invited to speak or make an appearance, I always try to be there, no matter where "there" might be. I am used to going the distance, quite literally: I've traveled to two different countries, thousands of miles apart, in the space of only a couple of days in order to be there for my fans and keep getting my message out to the world.

Turning down *The Doctors* that second time was not a decision I made lightly, but I knew that making a commit-ment like that would be too much for my schedule, my health, and my sanity. If I'd accepted, taping the episode would have happened right after another conference I was attending, and I knew from experience how draining that entire week would be. In the week following, I was scheduled to travel to two different cities in Bolivia and then to Miami right after that. All that airplane travel and interacting with fans would mean I was exposed to lots of different germs, which always increases my chances of getting sick. Going on the show simply wasn't a good idea.

Saying no was still so difficult, even though I knew it was the right thing to do. That was a big step for me: feeling the guilt, second-guessing myself, but doing it anyway, based on the deep conviction that it was the right thing to do.

That was part of my journey toward learning to say no without feeling guilty. Rest and relaxation also bring their own issues. I know I need at least a little time to relax each week, but making that time can be difficult. More than that, when I'm faced with spending a long, lonely day on my own, I often end up going a little stir-crazy, overthinking things and worrying that I'm wasting time I could be using to work.

Despite my uneasiness with downtime, I have started making it a point to take care of myself—a little time off here and there but also if I'm feeling anxious, instead of letting it sit, I will drop everything and take Ollie for a walk. Those thoughts are a terrible waste of time, and they distance you from the present moment. They cause guilt and self-blame, which are both hurtful and pointless.

That's why this is such an important process for everyone—learning to push through your guilt enough to put yourself first sometimes. It's definitely noble to strive not to embody those negative aspects of selfishness, at least not very often; but it's also noble to strive for the "good" kind of selfishness every now and again, too. After all, a certain type of selfishness allows us to refill our inner well, so we have enough energy and love to keep putting positivity out into the world.

I always say that creating positive change in the world

starts with just one person: you. That's why it is so important to learn to be the right kind of selfish. It's essential to learn the art of taking care of ourselves so that we can have the energy and the willpower to take care of each other and the world that we live in.

When you learn to love and take care of yourself, it becomes easier to turn your kindness outward, toward others. It becomes second nature to give people the benefit of the doubt, rather than judging them harshly. In the end, we all wish the world could be a kinder, gentler, and better place where we could all just coexist in peace, and we can, if we all make it a priority to take good care of ourselves.

CHAPTER 15

It's Up to Us

In the face of the world's many problems, some relatively small, some incredibly urgent and severe, it's easy to feel overwhelmed. Have you ever wished you could change something—something big—but you knew you couldn't do it by yourself? It's easy to feel defeated before you even begin to get a handle on how such important, large-scale changes can possibly be made. It's easy to wonder, "Where do I even start?"

But the answer to that question is actually pretty simple: You start with yourself.

I say this often, because it's true. If you want to change the world, you start small, right at home. You start with your family. You start with yourself, by embodying the change that you hope to see in the world around you.

The importance of being kind to one another and to ourselves can't be overstated, but it isn't always easy. Kindness takes energy, and I know how it feels to be overworked and dead tired at the end of the day. I know how it feels to deal with feelings of depression and anxiety. There might be days when you feel as if you don't have even a single drop left in your reserve tank to spread a little kindness.

Say you're at the grocery store, late in the evening, buying some milk and cereal for the next morning. All you want is to complete your purchase and get home so you can throw yourself into bed. The last thing you might feel like doing is smiling at the cashier or helping the woman in front of you who's just accidently spilled the contents of her purse onto the floor. She's holding up the line, and you just want her to get it together so you can get home already!

I get it. I really do. But kindness is something that can be practiced and built over time into a habit. And it's worth the effort. If you just push yourself to smile anyway and crouch down to help the woman gather her things, you're actually spreading a little joy. You'll feel better, she'll definitely feel better, and—*bam*—you've just made one tiny corner of the world a better place.

Seriously, even the smallest acts of kindness can mean everything. Do just one little thing to help someone out or make them feel special, and it can make their day or even change their life. It's like a ripple effect in a pond: Toss in a pebble, and the ripples extend outward, getting bigger and bigger. It's the same when you focus on compassion and helping others—even the smallest acts of kindness can have a big effect over time.

One way I've been practicing this in my own life is by giving random compliments to strangers I encounter out and about. Anytime I see something about someone that I like— maybe they're wearing a pretty scarf, or I like their hair or their smile—I make the effort to tell them. It's just a little thing, but random compliments can make someone's day!

In practicing this, I've discovered something surprising: Focusing on ways to spread a little joy can be a real relief, because it takes the spotlight off your own life.

This is especially true when you're in pain. If you suffer from depression or anxiety, or if you're grieving a loss, it can be easy to become rather self-absorbed. I don't mean this in a judgmental way; in my experience, it's simply true. There is a narrowing of focus that occurs. The more problems you have to shoulder, the tougher it becomes to pay attention to anything outside your own concerns. You just don't have the inner resources to deal with anything more than your own pain plus the bare minimum that is necessary to get through the day.

I've been there. I've had that narrowing of focus happen to me, when all I could think about were my own problems and my own pain. From going through my breakdown and coming out the other side, I know what it's like to feel so hopeless that you think it might be easiest for everyone if you just weren't around anymore. That is not true, of course. I can't stress it enough—that is a very serious error in thinking. But in those moments when you feel worthless and sick from the inside out, and you just want to find an escape route out of the pain, it's sometimes the only thing you can believe.

It is essential to deliberately turn your focus outward, away from your own problems, toward spreading joy to others. When you make a conscious effort to spread joy, you're also making the effort to step outside your own head—to stop thinking about yourself for a moment. What a relief that can be! You forget about your troubles or insecurities when you focus on someone else's feelings, and then you get the boost of knowing you made someone feel special, even if only for a moment.

I first encountered this idea on the *Bobby Bones Show*. He has a cohost, Amy, whose mother, Judy, died of cancer a few years ago. When Judy was first diagnosed, they wanted to do something to help other people in the same position, so they came up with a Twitter hashtag, #PimpinJoy. Initially, some people were turned off by the word *pimp*, but over time it caught on. They ended up founding Joy Week—the first week of every March, which is dedicated to doing random acts of kindness. The idea is to do something kind and unexpected for a stranger, whether it's something big or something small, and you tell them, "I'm pimpin' joy! All I ask is that you spread the joy to someone else."

When I first heard about Pimpin' Joy, I thought it was such a fantastic idea, I immediately decided to make it a part of my own life. On the *Bobby Bones Show*, they told stories about awesome acts of kindness during Joy Week, like entire lines of people in Starbucks drive-throughs who kept paying for the drinks of the people in the cars behind them, or a man who bought another customer a whole set of new tires at the tire store, all in the name of Pimpin' Joy. I thought that was the coolest thing! What a wonderful tribute to Amy's mother, Judy, and what an incredible contribution toward making the world a kinder, better, and more joyful place.

Of course, not everyone has enough money to buy a set

of new tires for a stranger or even to pay for someone else's mocha latte. But you don't have to spend a dime to spread joy. It can be as simple as giving someone a genuine smile, holding the door for them at the post office, or giving them a compliment. You can slip a note under the windshield wiper of someone's car that says, "This isn't a ticket—I just hope you have a wonderful day!" The good news is, there are no rules. Your acts of kindness can be as big or small, creative or simple as you'd like them to be.

I remember reading a story a while back in *People* magazine about a homeless man who donated 18 cents to a church. That was all the money he had in the world. It wasn't much, but the kindness and selflessness he displayed in making that donation astounds me. He had so much character, and he embodied the exact value I hold so dear: that the most important thing in life, above all, is helping others. We are here to help other people, and each and every one of us can harness the goodness inside us all.

I also believe that at the end of the day, what brings people joy is feeling connected. So make the effort to reach out and connect with someone. Let them know that you see them, you value them, and you're glad they're here. It could make all the difference.

———

All too often, we see stories in the news about people who commit terrible, unthinkable acts of cruelty. People like Adam Lanza, who murdered twenty-six people at Sandy Hook Elementary, including twenty schoolchildren. Or Elliot

Rodger, the teenager who opened fire at Santa Barbara City College, murdering six people and injuring fourteen others before turning his gun on himself and ending his own life. Or Omar Mateen, who murdered forty-nine people and injured fifty-three more inside an Orlando nightclub before police finally killed him after a three-hour standoff.

These stories seem to pop up in the news on almost a daily basis. Every time they do, I shudder inside. These atrocities make me feel physically ill. But every time there's a new, appalling headline in the paper, I can't help thinking about the kind of isolation and pain those young men must have been experiencing to do something so horrific. Even as my heart breaks for the families of the victims, I also can't help but think of the parents of the people who committed those terrible acts.

How must they have felt when the child they raised in the best way they knew how grew up to do something unspeakably vicious? They may have doted on their children when they were little and had big hopes and dreams for their futures. How crushing that must be—how completely shattering— to see all your hopes and dreams as a parent come crashing down around you in such a devastating way.

As uncomfortable as it is, it's important to consider what it might be like to be in those families' shoes. That's how we gain true understanding that we are all human—even those among us who commit the unthinkable. If we can really, truly see and understand that *we are all human*, we can develop empathy and kindness.

That's far easier to say than it is to do. But as tough as it is, parents across the country have to grapple with these issues, even when they never come anywhere close to home. I can only imagine how news stories like those might make a parent fear for their own children—not only that their children might someday become the victims of some awful, random crime, but also that if their child is misunderstood or in unspeakable pain, they might feel driven to hurt themselves or others.

I absolutely don't want to sound as if I'm making excuses for people who commit devastating acts of cruelty, but I can't help but think I might understand a little bit about their pain. My own personal faith has taught me to love the sinner, even as I hate the sin. I believe deeply in forgiveness and compassion, even for people who many would label monsters.

The simple, frightening truth is that no one is born wanting to kill people. I don't want to minimize the seriousness of mental illness, but some murderers and sociopaths are created through their experiences in life. Something happens in their lives that pushes them to the point of vicious cruelty. They reach a breaking point that makes them want to lash out in the most devastating way possible.

As a society, we are working to heal and treat people suffering from mental illness. Still, in cases where we can, there are ways to prevent tragedy long before it occurs, and I believe understanding kindness and compassion is the answer. We can do our part to take precautionary measures that might help prevent tragedies. Those people who are fueled by hatred and anger to lash out against others, what if they had experienced more kindness, compassion, and acceptance in their own lives? In many cases, their outcomes would have been different.

All of us, together, are responsible for creating a culture of kindness. When I think about my country and what it is to be an American, I feel a deep sense of pride. There are so many parts of our culture that are incredible. Americans are strong, independent, and resourceful. We prize freedom and equality.

But the truth is, certain aspects of our culture aren't so wonderful. As a society, generally speaking, we suffer from greed, entitlement, and an expectation of instant gratification. It's the fast-food culture: We want what we want, when we want it, and we don't want to have to wait—and we've gotten to the point where we can almost have that. Practically anything we might want, we can order it online and have it delivered to our door within an hour, or a day at most, as long as we can pay for it. We don't even like having to wait to watch a TV show anymore! If we want to know the score of a game or watch the latest episode of our favorite show, we can just pull out our smartphones and pull it right up.

I think of this as our "entitlement culture." Technological advances have brought us to a point in time when we can indulge our every whim, and that has created a certain kind of selfishness in us as a culture. And not the right kind of selfish, either! This is a toxic version of selfishness, a version that can make us forget we aren't the most important person in any given room. It's all too easy to lose touch with the fact that other people and their feelings and needs are just as important as our own.

On the other side of that same coin is our collective, rampant insecurities. We live in a materialistic culture that values outward signs of success, and we get caught up in trying to impress others with how fabulous we are. None of that is real, either. All of it is an illusion to create the appearance of beauty, strength, and confidence, but it's not genuine in the least.

Which brings us back to the importance of genuine self-confidence and the ability to truly love and value oneself. This is especially true for people who have some quality that is outwardly different from "the norm."

Some people might have a medical condition or a syndrome, like me. Others might have a disability of some kind. Still others might just be someone whom people would describe as "odd" or "quirky." Some of us are confident enough from the start to embrace our quirks, but for many of us, that's hard to do, and developing that inner strength is a process.

A huge part of why I put myself out there on social media and in my speeches and in my documentary is because *we are all different. And we are also all the same.*

What makes me different from most people is immediately visible, and my looks can seem shocking to some. I know some people still see me as the ugliest woman in the world, just like whoever posted that short little video of me on YouTube so long ago. But that just doesn't matter to me anymore, not nearly as much as it matters that I keep pushing to broaden people's perceptions of what's "normal." My work is about increasing our culture's acceptance of the fact that everybody is different. We are all different, and that's a good thing!

And people need to be exposed to those differences. There's been a lot of research done in this area, and the data seems to show that exposure is key. When people spend time with someone they see as being different from themselves, they end up feeling greater empathy toward that person after getting to know them a little. There is so much power in that—in having the opportunity to realize that, *Oh, you and I aren't actually all that different. Or, We're different, because everyone is a little different. And yet, we're also the same.*

The sea change I am calling for—the cultural shift I am trying to create? The end goal is for people to truly embrace each other's differences, as well as their own. Someday, I would love to see people all over the world start to realize it's not a dirty word to say you have a diagnosis or a disability or a syndrome, that it's perfectly fine to admit you're gay or lesbian or transgender or that you love dressing in drag. I would love to see people embrace each other for their qualities, like genetic variances, personality traits, physical characteristics, or inborn preferences, that stand out as being different in some way.

I would love to see humankind move toward accepting that it's truly okay to be different from the expected norm. Then I would love to see us abandon the entire concept of "the norm" once and for all. Because what is "normal," after all?

How wonderful would it be if the only expected norm could be, simply, kindness?

CHAPTER 16

This Is My Lottery

Have you ever won the lottery? Maybe you've purchased a scratch-off ticket or a Quick Pick at a convenience store and ended up winning a few dollars or maybe even a nice little windfall. Maybe you've never won the lottery or never even played. If you won, what is the greatest prize you could imagine?

For most people, the phrase "winning the lottery" conjures images of huge piles of cash. Imagine it: more money than you've ever had in your life, more money than you know what to do with!

Sounds great, right? I used to think so. But over time, I've learned that the greatest prize in life doesn't have to do with money or material wealth at all. It's about living and achieving your best possible life, flaws and all!

Over the past few years, I've had a crash course in living my own best possible life so far and in accepting my many flaws without apology. I'm certainly not perfect—but I'm not after perfection. Perfection is an impossible standard, one that can force people into a one-note way of being—a uniformity that's both boring and dangerous. I say perfection is boring because it chokes out all the wonderful, unique variations that make us the individuals that we are. And I say it is dangerous because it prevents people from celebrating and embracing those wonderful, unique variations.

Besides, we're all evolving, and that's life. That's what it's all about! The goal isn't to reach perfection but to keep striving and keep moving forward along our paths. The goal is also to stop and recognize the blessings and the beauty along the way, no matter where we might find ourselves along this path of personal and cultural evolution.

That's why our focus should not be on pursuing perfection. Instead, we should focus on striving for authenticity. Living your own, authentic truth, no matter what: That's what is meaningful.

In April 2016, I was honored to receive a Hispanicize Latinovator award. Since 2012, Latinovator awards have recognized Latinos with remarkable or inspirational stories of achievement. Winning the award put me in the ranks of such legendary past recipients as journalist Soledad O'Brien, actor Luis Guzmán, musician Sheila E., and many others. Rosario Dawson received a 2016 Latinovator award, too. I was in excellent company!

The award came at a point in my life that felt something like a pinnacle and yet something like a turning point as well. The documentary that had taken up nearly two full years of my life, along with a whole lot of blood, sweat, and tears, was now behind me. I'd reached my goal of joining a speakers' bureau and was looking forward to the changes that would surely come. I had moved on from a couple of significant relationships, and I was having fun dating casually.

Most of all, I was faced with the question of what to work on next. What would the next chapter of my life look like? For the first time, I unapologetically loved my life! It was authentic and uniquely mine. All of my wildest dreams were coming true...yet I was still wondering about the next chapter.

The next chapter is a question I consider regularly, and I hope I always will. I hope I never plateau; I hope I continue looking forward and setting my sights on new goals.

At the same time, it's important to appreciate the past, even when looking back isn't easy. The past can be a little overwhelming to take in, especially if you've been through a lot—but it's important to acknowledge the past in order to see where you are now. Even if you aren't exactly where you'd like to be, if you take a step back, I'll bet you can find glimpses of achievement in various areas of your life. I think we've all had more dreams come true than we might realize in any given moment.

Confronting our pasts can fill us with anxiety, just as much as looking forward to an uncertain future can. I know this all too well! Finally, though, I'm at a place where it's easier than ever to do both of those. At this point, I've learned simply to put up my hands and say, *Okay—wherever the universe leads me next, that's where I'll go.* No matter how nervous I might feel, I'm ready. At this point, I just don't have the energy to worry.

Getting to this point was a process. If you've ever been

through a traumatic event, I'm sure you can relate to trauma anniversaries being huge. A year after my breakdown, I kept having moments when I would realize it was exactly a year later. Suddenly, the particular slant of the sunlight or the color of the leaves on the trees would hit me, and I would realize with a jolt that the season was the same, the weather was the same, but I was in a completely different place in my heart and my life.

I'm lucky that the year following my breakdown turned out to be night-and-day different from the one that had led up to it, in the best way possible. I overcame a truly challenging phase, pushing through it toward better mental health. That still fills me with a great sense of pride. Even so, I've had to learn the hard way to prepare myself whenever I'm about to go through another major life transition, so I won't be caught unaware and risk another downward spiral.

The times when I could really see how far I'd come were those times when I was home alone in the year or so following my breakdown. I'd been experiencing significant back pain due to lots of travel for speaking engagements. My doctor had prescribed me pain medication, and there were moments when I would be alone in my apartment, and I would think about it: *I could take one.* Those thoughts would arise unbidden, and I would probe them for weakness, the way you might press at a bruise to see if it still hurts.

I was incredibly relieved to find the bruise had healed, at long last. Those thoughts flitted through my mind more than once, but each time, they simply evaporated. Several times, it was Ollie that brought me back to my senses. Just looking at him would inspire a soul-deep realization that I couldn't take a pill, not only because I couldn't do that to myself, but also because I couldn't do that to him. The last thing I wanted in the world was to put my family through that pain and uncertainty all over again. Most of all, I refused to step backward and put myself back in that place I'd struggled so hard to leave behind.

Fortunately, I had plenty of good things in my life to distract me. One came in the form of a weekend trip back to my mother's hometown. I'm so lucky: Because of my mom, the whole town of Gonzales considers me a local, and every time I go, they welcome me with open arms. When my documentary was released on DVD in January 2016, I did a DVD signing at the town's local Walmart, and it was so fun to see the crowd that turned out to welcome me and celebrate my movie.

My grandparents on my dad's side still live in Waelder, the town nearby where my father grew up. When we arrived at the Walmart in Gonzales for the DVD signing, they were there, right at the front of the line. I was set up at a table in the front of the store, and the line of people stretched all the way to the back. It was such an honor! There were over fifty copies of the film available for sale, and we sold out in less than an hour.

These are the people who keep me happy and sane. That's why I always try to let them know, in tangible ways, how much I care about them and appreciate them. I love doing things like treating my sister to a surprise day of pampering at the salon or hanging out with my brother, watching movies or just talking. When it comes to my parents, I don't even know how to start repaying them for all the years of love, help, and support they've given me. I've always said that one day I'll have a pool built for them in their backyard. When I was younger, we never went to public pools because people would stare at me and I felt uncomfortable. Many years later, we still talk about our dream home with a big, gorgeous pool out back. One of these days, I'm going to make that dream a reality for them.

I truly don't know what I would do without them, but I do know one thing: Whenever I do get the chance to give my parents their dream home, it won't be about giving them material things. It will be about showing my gratitude for their role in my life. Their love for me is authentic, it is special, and it could never be copied.

The concept of my life, as it is, being my winning lottery came from a wise friend named Christopher Roldan.

Chris was one of the editors of A Brave Heart. During the filming of the documentary, we hadn't had many chances to really get to know each other. After an early screening of the film in Los Angeles, it was time to head back to Austin, and Chris and I ended up flying together. He always made me laugh, and he had a way of teaching me a thing or two every time we chatted, so I was looking forward to sharing a flight back home.

Sure enough, he had me laughing from the moment the plane took off. After a while, the conversation turned more serious. We discussed my speaking career and my hopes to continue reaching more and more people with my message.

We talked about feeling that people truly are kinder nowadays than ever before.

Thanks to television and the Internet, it's easier than it has ever been in the course of human history to be aware of others' feelings and what others deal with on a day-to-day basis. It's easier than ever before to gain a window into the lives of people who are different from ourselves, which builds empathy. The terrible issue of cyberbullying is ironic in light of the fact that we also have the Internet to thank for allowing us to carry on a global conversation about bullying.

I told Chris I felt real progress was being made in our culture, and I told him of my hope to contribute to that progress.

"When the film comes out," he said, "it'll help you reach even more people than ever before."

The enormity of that really hit me, in that moment. I was excited about what was coming, but I was also conscious of a sense that I'd been given an enormous gift that I hadn't yet worked up the courage to open. I knew this opportunity to make a film about my life was a gift, but I couldn't be sure what might be inside, or whether I would like it, until I ripped off the wrapping.

It was exciting and scary all at once. It felt like balancing at the edge of a precipice. I could almost feel myself poised there, right at the brink, holding my breath before I took a swan dive into the unknown.

When I described that feeling to Chris, he responded by saying something that has stayed with me ever since.

"This is your lottery," he told me. "The good and the bad. For some people, winning the lottery means winning a million bucks. But for you, this is it: living out your dream to help people."

This is my lottery.

I turned the words over and over in my mind. This was my lottery: my life as a whole—everything that had happened to me, everything that was on the horizon, and most of all, becoming the person I'd always felt I was meant to be.

Chris was right. It wouldn't matter if a duffel bag full of cash suddenly fell right out of the sky and plopped down in the middle of my apartment balcony. I'd already won my lottery. I was living it, every single day.

I looked at him and grinned. "You're right. This is my lottery."

He smiled back, and then he pointed at me with a wink. "You can quote me on that."

I laughed. And then I took him at his word and quoted him, right here in the pages of this book.

This *is* my lottery.

I wrote this book in order to tell my story and spread my message, but I also wrote it for *you*—because you are awesome and amazing, and the world could not do without you. I want every person reading this book to know this: You play an important role in cocreating a kinder future. We can't do it alone; it takes every one of us, working together.

———

Whenever I have doubts about my life or my future, a recurring thought always pops into my mind: God's plan is bigger than mine. His plan is already laid out and waiting, so it's pointless for us to struggle as we try to make things unfold in a certain way. Rather than focusing on our own ideas of what we think would be the best, all we need to do is to enjoy the ride.

This has been a big lesson for me. As I've mentioned, I can be a bit of a control freak in certain areas of my life. A lifetime of dealing with health issues largely outside my control has given me the urge to take charge of any parts of my life that I can.

But when I get anxious about wanting things to go a certain way, it's so helpful to put up my hands and reconnect with my inner sense of faith that my life has already been planned out for me. It's not within my control, and it isn't supposed to be.

What a relief! With that simple realization, the burden is lifted off my shoulders. I can set goals and work toward them, but I don't have to strive toward any particular outcome. I can let go and simply let my life follow its course.

Our lives have already been planned, and it's a far greater plan than we could ever dream of. That is one of my deepest beliefs. It's a belief that has come from the teachings of my religion, but you don't have to be Catholic or even a person of religious faith to benefit from a similar point of view. There is so much peace to be found in reaching a point where you can let go and trust that you're on your path. Even if you're at a particularly bumpy spot in the road, there is a beautiful tranquility in trusting that you're exactly where you are supposed to be. We experience challenges in order to learn and grow. We have fears because we're human, and our life's work includes working through them, to come to a place of genuine self-acceptance, compassion, and love.

Many people, whether they are religious or spiritual, agnostic or atheistic, believe in the importance of personal evolution. As humans, as a species, we are meant to move away from selfishness and cruelty. Life should be about overcoming our egotistical, small-minded instincts and embracing the more open-minded, loving aspects of our nature.

But many people have no idea how to do that, simply because they've never experienced decency and kindness. All too often, kindness is seen as weakness, and that's a big problem. Many people are so afraid of being duped or overpowered that they behave cruelly in order to seem strong. People mistake force and anger for strength, when those couldn't be further from true strength.

There is good news, however. It can feel as if the world is a cruel and chaotic place, and if you pay any attention to the daily news, that feeling can be compounded exponentially. But that feeling isn't actually a reflection of reality. Overall, people are nicer now than we have ever been in the past. Despite what headlines would lead us to believe, violent crimes and homicide rates are decreasing, war is on the decline, and humans are becoming less sexist and less racist overall. Harvard psychology professor Steven Pinker actually wrote a book about these trends, in which he calls the present "the most peaceable era in our species' existence."

I see the Internet as being largely responsible for this shift. With the Internet, we truly have the world at our fingertips. Despite all the problems that can come with connecting online, doing so also allows us to be more aware of each other, including our differences, than ever before. The Internet also provides a great forum for carrying on global conversations about subjects like bullying, violence, and compassion.

Best of all, more and more often, I see people online speaking up for others, telling the bullies of the world, "That's not nice." Even young children are finding the strength to stand up for each other and stand together against bullies. This wasn't so prevalent just a few short years ago, but there is a growing awareness. There is progress.

People's comments on my YouTube channel are night and day from when I first started out a decade ago. The majority of comments these days are so nice and supportive! That gives me shivers, since it's a direct indication that what I set out to do is *really, actually happening*: I wanted to change the culture on the Internet, to make the Web a kinder place to be, and that's exactly what is occurring.

Most of my videos get plenty of thumbs-up clicks, but every once in a while, someone will click the thumbs-down. One of my favorite, ongoing jokes is when one of my viewers notices the handful of thumbs-downs on one of my videos and leaves a comment: "Uh-oh, six people accidentally clicked the wrong thumb!" That one never gets old! It cracks me up every time, and it's always a great reminder of what a caring, supportive—and hilarious—community we have built together online.

Granted, my YouTube channel and my other social media platforms amount to just one small corner of the Internet. But my little community is growing, and even a small corner of the Internet matters. To me, that is progress. And I only see that progress continuing in the future.

CONCLUSION

Dare to Be Kind:
A Call to Action

It is my hope that my story and this book are an inspiration to others. I also hope it's clear that the inspiration in all of our lives, in all our stories, doesn't lie only in the big, shining, triumphant moments. It also lies in the low moments, the rough ones, when we feel broken and beaten. I've had my share of thrilling highs as well as some appalling lows, and that's how life works for all of us: highs and lows, ups and downs. Without the downs, the ups wouldn't have much significance.

Whatever you're going through, whether you're experiencing bullying, dealing with anxiety or depression, or having dark thoughts, I have been there, too, and I've come through it in one piece. I want to serve as the voice or the light you need to help you reach a place of greater love and compassion for yourself and everyone around you.

You can win your own lottery. Yes, you can, even if you're

struggling right now! Maybe you have relationship problems or money trouble. Maybe you're dealing with a profound loss. Maybe you have a disability that makes your life harder than you wish it could be.

Whatever you are dealing with, that is your lottery. Challenges are your opportunity to learn, grow, and become the person you're meant to be. And you can do it. I know you can! No matter what you are struggling with, whether it's something heavy and ongoing or just a few bad days, there's a way to get through it. There's always a way to get through it. You have the strength and resilience within yourself to thrive.

You may not believe that... yet. I realize that it may seem conveniently easy for me to write that in the pages of a book. Things always wrap up nicely and prettily in books and movies, right? But that's not realistic. It's not the way life is. Terrible things can still happen. Bad things happen to good, kind, honest, and hardworking people every day. It's unfortunate, but it's simply true. Sometimes you put in your very best effort, and things still fall apart.

When things go wrong in our lives, what matters is how we deal with it. The pain that comes from changes and endings is all about loss: loss of a relationship, of a pet, of a beloved family member; loss of a job, money, or a comfortable, familiar identity. Transitions like these are difficult because they represent a loss, so we must have methods in place to process the loss and move forward from it. That requires seeing not only what has been lost, but also what has been gained.

Of course, if you're in the midst of a crisis, seeing the silver lining can feel absolutely impossible. You might feel as if you couldn't be further from winning your lottery, and strength and resilience might seem like little more than a cruel joke. That's why I urge you to start simple: Start with kindness, and start with yourself. Dare to be as good to yourself as you would be to someone you truly loved—because that's how you should feel about yourself. Dare to treat yourself as a dear and precious friend.

Then, when you're ready, dare to turn your kindness outward into the world. Bathe the world in your warmth and compassion. Shower the people you encounter with love and acceptance. But don't stop there! If each and every one of us commits to taking these steps, little by little, we will change the world into a place where there is no fear of difference, and no fear of cruelty or harassment. In flooding this world with love, we will be taking active steps toward creating a better future for our children and a better culture for everyone—a culture of kindness.

Acknowledgments

This book is without a doubt my dream book. There are many people who helped bring it to life and I will be forever grateful to each of them. To my parents, the people who built such an incredible foundation of faith, courage, and support for me. It is my honor to be your daughter. To my siblings Chris and Marina. Thank you both for being my best friends. Thank you for going to get late-night fast food with me when I was up late working and needed a break. Even though you both think I lie around all day in my pajamas, I love you so much.

To the two women who have helped me step into my own as a young lady. Sara Hirsch Bordo and Jessica Chou, there aren't enough words to express how much you have changed my life. Thank you for holding my hand on the days when I needed it most. Thank you for giving me the courage to live life without any crutches.

To my incredible writing partner, Catherine Avril Morris. Thank you for being the best "book mom" a girl could ask for. Thank you for your patience and encouragement during our writing process. From working with my hectic schedule to the sessions when I wasn't feeling my best. You taught me so much and I am a better writer because of you.

Big thanks to my amazing book team and family at Waxman Leavell and Hachette Books. Thank you so much, Cassie Hanjian, Krishan Trotman, and Mauro DiPreta. Thank you for believing in my message and giving me the platform to share it.